MW01134504

Grape Juice in the Bible: God's Blessing for His People!

Richard Teachout

biblical.grape.juice@gmail.com

These were more noble than those in Thessalonica,
in that they received the word with all readiness of mind, and searched the
scriptures daily, whether those things were so. (Act. 17:11)

Prove all things; hold fast that which is good. (1 Th. 5:21)

Major revision and updating of
On the Fruit of the Vine: In Defense of Biblical Consistency (2010)
By the same author© 2011 Richard Teachout
Cover graphics by Debra King
Texture behind grapes/wine glass: www.aldonscott.com
Texture behind title: none requested
Bible: Cíntia Martins

Published by:
EBPA - Etude Biblique pour Aujourd'hui (Bible Studies for Today)
8890, boul. Ste-Anne
Chateau-Richer, QC G0A1N0
Canada

(418) 827 -9012
www.ebpa-publications.org
info@ebpa-publications.org

EBPA is a small missionary-run donations-based ministry of publication, providing needed literature and tools to help with evangelism and discipleship, mainly for French speaking mission fields.

ISBN 978-2-9811211-9-6

Legal deposit:
    National Library of Canada
    Bibliothèque nationale du Québec

To my late father,

who taught me that

God always speaks the truth to us

And

that He always speaks consistently

in His Revelation.

To my brother,

who in modern times

pioneered the scholarship

which finds God's teaching

about the fruit of the vine in the Bible

to be consistent.

To my wife Nancy and my son Raymond,
for their help and encouragement,
and without whom this project
would never have been completed.

Table of Contents

Introduction

I preached a series of four messages in October 2010 on "Wine in the Bible." My purpose was to enlighten Christians to the truth that God never encourages His children to partake of an alcoholic beverage. The third message, "God Blesses Grape Juice in the Bible," became the most important in that series. In that message I show from the Word of God that, contrary to almost all Bible expositors of our day, grape juice did indeed exist in Bible times. At the conclusion I asked and answered the question, "Does it matter?" Does it matter whether God's people in Bible times had only alcoholic wine to drink or rather that they had a choice between that and natural grape juice with no alcoholic content?

I realized at that point just how much it mattered, for this is the key to the entire debate on Christians drinking alcohol in our time. I decided to rewrite the book *On the Fruit of the Vine, In Defense of Biblical Consistency* which I had written earlier in the year. I feel that the erroneous idea that grape juice is not mentioned in the Bible is why conservative Christians en masse have so drastically changed their teaching on alcohol in the last 50 years.

The result of the aggressive promotion of this erroneous teaching is that there has been a major push in recent times to promote an interpretation of Scripture that would affirm that Jesus Himself created an alcoholic beverage in His first miracle and drank of it Himself. Since He did this, we can too! The result is a major shift in Christian thought – more and more are promoting or condoning a Christian's right to drink alcohol. One startling manifestation of this is detailed in the following article. After 68 years of teaching and practicing abstinence, a former fundamentalist Bible college has changed its policy on moderate drinking! Why? Because they now interpret the Bible to say that God permitted and encouraged it! Their president asserted that alcohol abstinence is "biblically indefensible." The same article goes on to name nine other Christian colleges which have taken the same position.[1] Other church leaders have gone even further. Mark Driscoll, who is pastor of the Seattle-area Mars Hill Church and president of the "Acts 29" group of churches, wrote in his book, *Radical Reformission,* that abstinence from alcohol is a sin.[2]

Though the modern message concerning alcohol has changed, the Bible has not changed its message. The Bible still affirms clearly that all Scripture is inspired of God and is profitable for His children (II Timothy 3:16). It is an absolute truth, fundamental to the Christian faith that God has spoken to man by His Word.

Can this God lie or fail to communicate clearly with His creatures? Absolutely NOT. A.W.Tozer said that worship rises or falls with our concept of God. If there is one terrible disease in the Church of Christ today, it is that we do not see God as great as He is. We're too familiar with God. I can further state here that our understanding of God's Word rises or falls with our concept of God. He is the great and wonderful creator God of the universe. He has spoken to man. He says that in His Word 300 times! Amos 4:13 says, *"For, lo, He that formeth the mountains, and createth the wind, and declareth unto man what is His thought,.. The LORD, The God of hosts, is*

THE GRAND RAPIDS

PRESS

SATURDAY, NOVEMBER 21, 2009

'Thou shalt not drink' revoked

Cornerstone University ends 68-year-old ban on imbibing for faculty, staff

BY KYM REINSTADLER
THE GRAND RAPIDS PRESS

GRAND RAPIDS — Cornerstone University is lifting a ban on faculty and staff alcohol use that has stood since the institution was founded 68 years ago.

President Joe Stowell told Cornerstone's 279 employees at a staff meeting Friday that alcohol abstinence — a component of a lifestyle statement that had to be signed every year — is being dropped because a three-year internal study concluded it is "biblically indefensible."

"Given scripture's lack of a prohibition against use of alcohol in moderation, we are releasing our faculty and staff to discern what is best for them concerning its use in their personal lives," said Stowell, in his second year as the university's president.

The change doesn't apply to students, who remain banned from using alcohol.

Faculty and staff are being told to avoid using alcohol in any setting where students are present. Corner-

Joe Stowell

MORE
• Cornerstone cuts staff

---

[1] *The Grand Rapids Press*, Nov 21, 2009, front page, article by Kym Reinstadler, reproduced by permission.
[2] Norm Miller, *Alcohol, Acts 29 and the SBC.* Posted on Mar 20, 2007 http://www.bpnews.net/bpfirstperson.asp?id=25221 (Accessed 6/23/2011).

His name."

We must understand that God's Word NEVER contradicts itself. So, how can God be inconsistent in His revelation concerning alcoholic beverages? Can He say in His Word that they are both good and bad, as some would understand today?

At the present time, there are three popular positions in America concerning Christians and alcoholic beverages:

1. Christians can partake of alcoholic beverages moderately and ONLY moderately, because God's people partook moderately in Bible times.
2. God's people partook moderately in Bible times but Christians should not do so today; they should abstain.
3. God's Word is not clear – we dare not speak to the issue, either for or against moderate drinking by Christians.

The first two positions are the subject of many articles, messages, and internet blogs. They both interpret God's Word in such a way that He blesses and condones the same substance, alcoholic wine. Proponents of both positions assert that grape juice is not found in the Bible and did not exist as a beverage in Bible times, because there was no way to preserve it. Position #3 is usually held by those who believe that abstinence is the best policy for Christians, but they do not have an answer to what they perceive as God's seeming inconsistency in blessing and condemning the drinking of "wine." Therefore the subject of wine in the Bible is something which is rarely discussed in fundamentalist and conservative evangelical churches though many of these churches have written policies prohibiting the use of alcoholic beverages for members.

The result is foreseeable and is being quickly realized. Something new is growing in American Christianity: tolerance (and often promotion) of the consumption of alcohol. The result is that the alcoholic beverage industry is entering into our Christian community like a camel which, once his nose is thrust into the tent, soon follows it with his body. This camel is very dangerous. This will be discussed later, but in the meantime consider this:

- ✓ Drug Experts Say Alcohol Worse Than Crack or Heroin.[3]
- ✓ Study: Alcohol 'most harmful drug,' followed by crack and heroin.[4]
- ✓ LONDON -- Alcohol is more dangerous than illegal drugs like heroin and crack cocaine, according to a new study.[5]
- ✓ Alcohol-related deaths account for almost 100,000 deaths per year in US.[6]
- ✓ WHO Reports that Alcohol-Related Deaths Kill More Than AIDS, TB Or Violence.[7]
- ✓ Alcohol dependence and alcohol abuse cost the United States an estimated $220 billion in 2005. This dollar amount was more than the cost associated with cancer ($196 billion) and obesity ($133 billion).[8]
- ✓ The 25.9% of underage drinkers who are alcohol abusers and alcohol dependent drink 47.3% of the alcohol that is consumed by all underage drinkers.[9]
- ✓ By the age of 16, most kids will have seen 75,000 ads for alcohol. Young people view 20,000 commercials each year, and nearly 2,000 are for beer and wine.[10]
- ✓ Each year, the alcohol industry spends more than a billion dollars on "measured media" advertising.[11]

---

[3] Published November 01, 2010, Reuters, http://www.reuters.com/article/2010/11/01/us-drugs-alcohol-idUSTRE6A000O20101101, (Accessed 7/7/2011).

[4] *Medical News Today*, http://www.medicalnewstoday.com/articles/206300.php, (Accessed 7/7/2011).

[5] MARIA CHENG, *The Associated Press*, Sunday, October 31, 2010; 8:08 PM, http://www.washingtonpost.com/wp-dyn/content/story/2010/11/01/ST2010110101970.html, (Accessed 7/7/2011).

[6] http://www.come-over.to/FAS/alcdeath.htm, (Accessed 7/7/2011).

[7] http://www.huffingtonpost.com/2011/02/11/alcohol-related-deaths-_n_821900.html, (Accessed 7/7/2011).

[8] http://www.alcoholism-information.com/Alcoholism_Statistics.html, (Accessed 7/7/2011).

[9] *Ibid.*

[10] http://www.ecstasyaddiction.com/PressReleasePages/therealcostofalcoholadvertising.html (Accessed 4/15/2011).

This then is the product that so many Christian preachers and scholars either promote or refuse to condemn, and this is what (according to so many modern writers) Jesus, the LORD of the universe, created and drank at Cana!

On the other hand, there are an increasing number of Christian ministers and writers who do not promote this product and condemn moderate drinking for Christians without reserve. A very recent posting on the internet is to be commended:

> *It would be an uphill battle merely to advocate moderation in drinking as many conservatives do, but to come to a conclusion that total abstinence is a Biblical mandate, would place one immediately in the backwater of Christian social fellowships. But that is just the conclusion I've come to, not just because I find it the overwhelming norm of Christian history, or because the statistics on drinking grow increasingly alarming, but because I've become convinced that this is the only consistent biblical teaching.*[12]

This book will deal with the fact that God clearly blesses grape juice in the Bible. Also, the subject of alcohol consumption will be considered at length, for it is inconceivable that the Holy Righteous God would not teach His children clearly about this subject. The great many inconsistencies that are being taught today will be pointed out as will contradictions in the TEACHING of modern Bible scholars on this subject. Here are some of the differences that will be examined:

Some say:	Other Godly Bible scholars affirm the contrary:
The Bible never mentions grape juice, the word "wine" only refers to an alcoholic beverage.	The Bible speaks often of both grape juice and fermented wine, blessing the juice and clearly condemning the alcohol.

---

[11] http://www.ftc.gov/reports/alcohol/appendixb.shtm (Accessed 4/15/2011).

[12] http://www.aletheiabaptistministries.org/ (accessed 9/2/2011).

The Bible permits alcoholic drinks for God's people.	The Bible condemns alcoholic drinks for God's people.
The Bible permits only moderate drinking of alcoholic beverages for God's people.	The Bible condones no drinking of alcoholic beverages for God's people.
The Bible says that Jesus created and drank "wine," an alcoholic beverage.	Jesus could not have created or drunk a product that causes such harm.
There was no safe drinking water in Palestine, and people had to mix an alcoholic beverage with water to make it safe.	There is no biblical, archaeological, or scientific proof for this. The Bible reveals God's instructions for good sanitation and abounds with references to drinking water.

How can this be? How can there be such a huge difference in understanding of the meaning of a Biblical word? Chapter X will extensively chronicle great shifts in attitude towards consumption of alcohol in just 150 years here in the United States, both in society as a whole and especially in the Christian community. It can be briefly said here that society moved from having a majority who were convinced of the evil of drinking and worked very hard at combating it to the present era where the evil of drinking has been accepted as normal in society and the youth lead the way in "pushing the envelope." The Christian community went from preaching and teaching against the use of alcoholic beverages to the present situation in which many evangelical leaders promote moderate consumption, where most evangelicals neither fight it nor teach against it, and where very few evangelical churches aggressively practice abstinence. Furthermore, the teaching that grape juice is in the Bible is attacked by all but a very few Bible scholars.

How can there be so many serious contradictions in God's inspired Word as those found in the debate on "wine" in the Bible? I would affirm and insist that there are no contradictions in God's Word nor can there be. There are only contradictions in our interpretation or understanding of it. We must start with the assurance and conviction that each

> *There are no contradictions in God's Word nor **can there be!***

scriptural thought or word is to be interpreted or understood in such a way that it can only complete and harmonize with the rest of Scripture. To be true to Himself, God must be consistently speak the same truth throughout His revelation! Therefore, in the case of the word "wine" in the Bible, we must work to find out what this word meant to its writers and readers in Bible times. Then we must apply that truth in our own lives, for *"whatsoever things were written aforetime were written for our learning, that we through patience and comfort of the scriptures might have hope"* (Rom 15:4). "Hope" here does not mean wishful thinking but "joyful and confident expectation." Jeremiah speaks of God as being the hope of Israel (Jer 17:13). The Psalmist says, "Happy *is he* that *hath* the God of Jacob for his help, whose hope *is* in the LORD his God" (Ps 146:5). Our hope is more than salvation. It includes all that God has promised us of His blessing and protection in our lives. Our "hope" is absolutely vain if God does not speak objective truth, if He does not mean what He says. This hope can only be realized by accepting ALL that the Bible says and putting it into practice.

The polemic and the public verbal sniping on the juice-wine issue has exponentially increased in our time. However, the central issue, the necessity of understanding God's Word always to be consistent, has always been clearly upheld by faithful men of God, even in reference to grape juice in the Bible. For instance, it was stated in several addresses by Eliphalet Nott, president of Union College in the early 1800's:

8

Can the same thing in the same state be good and bad, a symbol of wrath, a symbol of mercy, a thing to be sought after, a thing to be avoided? Certainly not!

And is the Bible then inconsistent with itself? No it is not, and this seeming inconsistency will vanish, and the Bible will be not only, but will appear to be in harmony with itself, in harmony with history, with science, and with the providence of God, if, on examination, it shall be found that the kinds or states of vinous beverage referred to, under the name of wine, were as unlike in their nature or effects, as were those mercies and judgments for which the same were respectively employed as symbols, or as were those terms of praise or dispraise by which the same were respectively indicated [13]

Let us continue our study with the goal of understanding what God has to say about grape juice and alcoholic beverages. In order to do this, I feel I must share some of my experiences which have helped me in my search for the answers to the problem and have contributed to my present conclusion.

[13] Eliphalet Nott, *Lectures on Temperance*, NEW-YORK: SHELDON, BLAKEMAN & CO., 115 NASSAU STREET, 1857, pp. 53,54.

I.   A Personal Problem with Alcohol

My personal problem with alcohol did not consist of using it or becoming a slave to it. Instead, it was, as I got older, an increasing uneasiness concerning what was being taught in Bible schools on the subject and how that affected my ministry.

Early Personal History

I grew up in a home where the use of alcohol was a non-issue. We firmly believed that alcohol had no place in a Christian's life. I stayed with a Christian farmer and his wife in Pennsylvania during my high-school years when my parents (who were missionaries) went back to Africa. No one that I knew in the church would have thought that alcoholic beverages had any place at all in a Christian home. Every single Sunday dinner was accompanied by a radio program from Pacific Garden Mission in Chicago called "Unshackled." Most of their programs at that time were stories of professional men with families who started out with light or moderate social drinking and then went on to finally become down-and-out bums on skid row where they found the Savior and gave up their alcohol. I had no desire whatsoever to try alcohol for myself. After high school, I went to a fundamentalist Baptist seminary and then went into the Marine Corps, where alcohol was a major problem. Throughout this time I was convinced that God did not condone alcohol for the Christian, but I would have been unable to answer the question about a Christian's right to drink alcohol because I had accepted what was taught in Bible School.

My wife was brought up in a dysfunctional home because of an alcoholic father. Without going into details, she was the only one of the family who graduated from high school and then college. She had found the Lord during grade school, and He preserved her in a very bad situation. Naturally, she has a strong aversion to any alcoholic beverage.

We met while I was still in the service, married, and started a family. After three more years in the Marines, including a stint in Vietnam, I mustered out of military service. During all my time in the USMC, I was never in the least tempted to taste any alcoholic beverage, though it literally flowed around me. My worst experiences during that time were seeing young marines from good families start in moderately with alcohol and then go quickly downhill toward destruction in sinful practices.

I left the military in order to go back to seminary and finish the last year of a five-year Th.B. degree. During that year the Lord called us to the mission field. After that, I finished three years of graduate study in order to set up a seminary in the Central African Republic where we felt God was leading us.

Alcoholic Beverages and Christians in Africa and France

After I finished graduate school, we went on to the Central African Republic and worked there seven years. In those churches, consumption of alcohol was not a problem. When people accepted the Lord, they left their former habits, which had included much consumption of alcoholic beverages. On Saturday evenings, from miles around, we could hear the drums and the dances going on in the villages. The people were stimulated and maintained by local alcoholic beverages leading to all sorts of sexual debauchery. Those who accepted the gospel did not consider mixing their former slavery to sin and their new freedom in Christ.

After seven years in Africa, we began our ministry in France. It was a completely different scene from Africa. Before we went to Africa, we had spent a year in France learning the French language, and thus we understood very well the part that wine has in the French culture. We knew that most French Christians, just like their fellow citizens, unfortunately consider that a meal without wine is not civilized.

We knew that several American misconceptions of how alcoholic beverages are consumed by French Christians were simply untrue. We had been told that the French drink wine because "they cannot get water that is safe to drink," but in France, wherever alcoholic beverages are sold, bottled water is always available – and much cheaper. We were also told that French Christians always dilute their wine to safe levels. This is simply not true. Sometime after we had moved from France to Quebec, we went back to visit. We were invited to a Christian wedding reception that was attended by many who had been part of our former youth group and where the bride and groom also had been in our youth group. We knew most of the participants and guests well and were terribly saddened to see the wine flow. In America a breathalyzer test would have kept them all from driving home legally. We decided then and there to never again attend a reception where alcohol would be served.

I had served in France for seven years as pastor of a church. One biblical subject we did not touch while in France was "wine" in the Bible. We had been told, by a veteran missionary on our arrival, that one must never tell a French Christian that one did not drink wine because of "principles" or "biblical convictions." Some other reason needed to be advanced. We should not question their culture which is very important to them.

During our time in France and in that church, we never accepted a drink and never had wine in our youth activities (though this would have been the norm if I had not been the pastor), but I respected the protocol and never taught why the subject of "wine" in the Bible was important. I have felt badly since I left there that I had not been faithful to God in this respect. I did later give a copy of my book in French on the subject to each of the young people with whom I had had a teaching relationship.

A Myth about "Wine" in the Bible Explodes

During my time in France, a myth was exploded for me, and my thinking was radically changed concerning "wine" in the Bible. I had always believed that it was wrong for a Christian to drink alcohol, but I had been taught in Bible school that the reason "wine" in the Bible had to be an alcoholic beverage was simply and irrefutably that there was no way to preserve grape juice as such in a hot climate. I had accepted this so irrevocably that I had simply laid aside a book I had read, a book which gave a clear teaching concerning "wine" in the Bible, expounding the same view that I now hold. Though this book was well written and soundly researched, it simply would not compute with what I had been taught. I had accepted the "fact" that wine in the Bible could not be anything but an alcoholic beverage since one could NOT preserve fresh grape juice in Biblical times.

Then one day my neighbor, who was not a Christian but who knew me well, offered me a drink of grape juice in his cellar. It was August and well before the harvest time for his grapes. I knew he had grapevines in his garden and that he always made his own juice. I looked at him. He said, "I know you do not drink wine. This is grape juice from my garden."

I said (stupidly), "*You kept it from last fall?*" He said, "*Bien sur*" (of course).

I asked, "*How?*"

He said, "*I bring it to a boil, put it in a jug, put a cork in it and leave it in my unheated cellar.*" I let him know that I was surprised. Then, wanting to know specifically if grape juice could be conserved an entire year, from harvest to harvest, I asked him if I could have a drink from the same jug of last year's juice after his new grape juice was made; he promised to call me at that time, and did. Wow! What a shock! That which I had been told, taught, and believed, simply was not true! Grape juice COULD be kept fresh all year long with very minimum effort! From this point in my life I began to study the subject in earnest. It would take a few years, but my "problem" of not understanding what God has to say about grape juice would finally disappear.

Alcoholic Beverages and Christians in French Quebec

Now I will resume the story of my "reeducation." I did not have the possibility of teaching on this matter during the rest of my stay in France. We went to Quebec, Canada, where I taught in a Baptist theological school and pastored Baptist churches for 20 years. During our early years there we saw a great shift in practice in the churches. Wine is not the usual alcoholic beverage in Quebec, though alcoholic consumption (beer) is a real problem in their society. When the gospel first entered freely into Quebec in 1948 and churches were started, being "saved" was also to be delivered from alcohol. That was what was practiced and taught in the new churches that were established.

Unfortunately, within a few decades this situation changed, and alcohol was being tolerated for use by more and more Christians. In a very short while, the majority of Quebecker Christians were following English Christians in Canada and America toward allowing moderate alcoholic consumption. Only a small number of churches in Quebec continued to teach total abstinence. The change was rapid and a response was needed. I wrote a book on the subject, "Le vin, la Bible, et le Chrétien" which translates in English as "Wine, the Bible, and the Christian." My goal was to offer Christians solid Biblical proofs of God's consistent teaching on abstinence. These are the proofs I had not had in my earlier ministry but had so desperately needed.

During my entire ministry in these three foreign countries, my contact with America was infrequent, being limited to brief visits to my supporting churches. When I moved back to the U.S. and began my present ministry, I became aware of the tremendous change in the attitude of the Christian community toward alcohol. This change is detailed in Chapter X. I also became aware of the aggressive teaching detailed in the Introduction: "The Bible never mentions grape *juice; the word "wine" only refers to an alcoholic beverage"*. I found good churches that had in their church constitutions statements about abstinence for their members, but the practice was much different. Actual practice was: "the less said about this – the better." Finally, I found that the number of Christians who drank alcohol and who defended their right to do so was increasing dramatically. This reality convinced me to pursue the study which has resulted in this book.

II.   A Key Problem of Interpretation

The popular and universal understanding of the English word "wine" in the Bible at the present time is that it always refers to an alcoholic beverage. This is NOT my understanding of the meaning of this word in Scripture, for this word in Scripture often means grape juice. How can this be? How can there be such a tremendous difference in the understanding of one word in the English Bible?

The specific problem of understanding what God says about grape juice and wine in the Bible is that the English translation for three Hebrew words and one Greek word is just one word, "wine." In modern English the word "wine" always means an alcoholic beverage. Our understanding of "wine" is, therefore, colored by our American culture.

And yet, the answer to this specific problem of interpretation is as simple as the problem is complex: the word "wine" in the English Bible as it was translated in the 17th century is generic: something that is general, common, or inclusive rather than specific, unique, or selective. This means it is one word which can mean at least two things, both grape juice and fermented wine. The word "water" is an example of this, for we have to specify salt water, fresh water, hard water, unsafe drinking water, etc. to express fully our meaning.

Another very good example of a generic word is the English word "cider." Cider is the juice pressed from fruits (apples, for example) which can be used for drinking or making other products such as vinegar. When I was a teenager on a farm in Pennsylvania, we made it and drank it every year, and it had NO alcoholic content. Yet for many, apple cider is "hard cider," made from apple juice, but fermented. Wikipedia says that *the unmodified term cider is generally assumed to refer to unfiltered apple juice,* but we know that one has to be careful, for in some restaurants if you ask for cider, you will receive "hard" cider.

The English word "wine" in the Bible is just such a generic word meaning the fruit of the vine in either form, grape juice and fermented wine. We will prove that here by looking at four different arguments.

1. That there is grape juice in the Bible is evident from Scriptural context

The truth that the English word "wine" is generic and has several meanings is seen from the fact that although there are cases where "wine" must mean an alcoholic beverage because of the clear context, there are also a great number of allusions to "wine" throughout Scripture which are clearly presenting unfermented grape juice. Here are a few of these: 1. "wine" is spoken of as the fruit of the land (Deuteronomy 7:13), which is grape juice. Fermented wine is man-made, by a process; it is not a natural process. 2. "Wine" in the Bible is often said to be furnished "out of the winepress" (Deuteronomy 15:14), but that which is pressed out of grapes in the press is, of course, grape juice. 3. The word "winepress" is found 14 times in the Bible and obviously means "grape press;" they would gather its product in with their corn and their oil (Deuteronomy 11:14); "their presses would burst out with it" (Proverbs 3:10); "the treaders shall tread out no wine in their presses" (Isaiah 16:10). One very clear reference to fresh grape juice is Isaiah 65:8 where God says: "Thus saith the LORD, as the new wine is found in the cluster, and one saith, Destroy it not; for a blessing is in it...." This means the fresh juice that is in the bunches of grapes.

2. That there is grape juice in the Bible is evident from other languages which translate Hebrew words for "wine" as grape juice

While it may not seem perfectly clear in our English Bible, sometimes other languages have made the obvious distinction between juice and alcohol. In Isaiah 65:8, the English Bible says: "*As the new wine is found in the cluster,*" but the French Bible (Louis Segond) says:

"Quand il se trouve du jus dans une grappe..." which means in English, *"When juice is found in a bunch of grapes..."* Obviously there is no fermented wine in a cluster or bunch of grapes!

The Hebrew word *"yayin"*, used most often in the Old Testament for the fruit of the vine, is generic and is rendered "wine" in our English Bible. The two principal words after *yayin* are *tirosh* (38 times) and *asis* (5 times). The French Bible translates *tirosh* by moût (must) most of the time, and *asis* as such every time. The principal meaning of these is not generic, but refers specifically to "must" or fresh grape juice. Since we will be using the English word *must* which is a little known word in present-day English, we will define it:

> **Must** *(from the Latin vinum mustum, "young wine") is freshly pressed fruit juice (usually grape juice) that contains the skins, seeds, and stems of the fruit... Making must is the first step in winemaking. Because of its high glucose content, typically between 10 and 15%, must is also used as a sweetener in a variety of cuisines.*[14]

It is clear that the word moût in French and *must* in English can only mean unfermented grape juice. The foremost French dictionary, *Larousse*, defines moût as: "unfermented grape juice which constitutes the raw material for winemaking." Here are some of the places in the Bible where *tirosh* is used:

> All the best of the oil, and all the best of the wine ("tirosh," lit. unfermented grape juice), and of the wheat, the firstfruits of them which they shall offer unto the LORD, them have I given thee, Num. 18:12.

> And this your heave offering shall be reckoned unto you, as though it were the corn of the threshing floor, and as the fulness ("tirosh," lit. unfermented grape juice) of the winepress, Num. 18:27.

---

[14] http://en.wikipedia.org/wiki/Must (Accessed 9/08/2011).

And he will love thee, and bless thee, and multiply thee: he will also bless the fruit of thy womb, and the fruit of thy land, thy corn, and thy wine ("tirosh," lit. unfermented grape juice), and thine oil, the increase of thy kine, and the flocks of thy sheep,... Deut. 7:13.

Israel then shall dwell in safety alone: the fountain of Jacob shall be upon a land of corn and wine ("tirosh," lit. unfermented grape juice); also his heavens shall drop down dew, Deut. 33:28.

There are several books available that examine each scriptural reference to "wine" and show how the context reveals the meaning (see bibliography). It is simply unscholarly to assert, as many modern writers do, that grape juice did not exist in ancient times and that it is not mentioned in the Bible.

3. That there is grape juice in the Bible is evident from historical dictionary definitions

The problem in understanding the original meaning of the Biblical word "wine" is often caused by the fact that the English usage of the word "wine" has changed from that which was current in the 17th century in English, French, and Latin. Samuel Bacchiocchi says, after citing several sources:

The above sampling of definitions of "wine" from older English dictionaries suggests that when the King James Version of the Bible was produced (1604-1611) its translators must have understood "wine" to refer to both fermented and unfermented wine.[15]

Actually there are several books which show the undeniable fact that the Hebrew and Greek words for "wine" and their English and

---

[15] Samuel Bacchiocchi, *Wine in the Bible: A Biblical Study on the Use of Alcoholic Beverages*, p. 58. Please note that we do not endorse the fact that Bacchiocchi is a Seventh-day Adventist.

French translations have, down through history, been generic words referring to the fruit of the vine and what is done with it. Baker says: "On this point there can be little argument; it is certain that people in the ancient world drank grape juice, and *oinos* was sometimes used to refer to fresh, non-alcoholic wine." [16] Robert Teachout says:

> *Long before the controversy over the prohibition against wine began in England and America, a large Latin lexicon, Thesaurus Linguae Latinae, (1740 A.D.) entered the fray. Volume 4, p.557, gave several definitions for vinum [wine], all supported by ancient Roman texts, including 'fresh grape juice,' 'bottled grape juice' and 'grape juice (vinum) so called while it was still in the unpressed grape.'* [17]

This generic use of the word wine or the French word "*vin*" can also be shown from older English, Italian and French dictionaries. *Webster's Revised Unabridged Dictionary* (1828 and 1913) gave this primary meaning: *1. The expressed juice of grapes, esp. when fermented; a beverage or liquor prepared from grapes by squeezing out their juice, and (usually) allowing it to ferment.* [18] If the fact that the words for wine in the Bible are generic is accepted, then it is easy to understand in any Biblical context exactly what God is saying. If He blesses its production or use, He is talking about unfermented grape juice. If He condemns or curses its use, He is referring to the alcoholic beverage.

4. That there is grape juice in the Bible is evident from Bible stories

One of the most striking examples of "wine" in the Bible being non-fermented concentrated grape juice is found in 1 Samuel 25:18:

---

[16] www.churchhistory101.com/docs/Wine-Ancient-World.pdf. (Accessed: 10/3/2009).
[17] Robert Teachout, *Wine the Biblical Imperative: Total Abstinence*, p. 21.
[18] http://machaut.uchicago.edu/?resource=Webster%27s&word= wine&use1913=on& use1828=on (Accessed 10/29/09).

Then Abigail made haste, and took two hundred loaves, and two bottles of wine, and five sheep ready dressed, and five measures of parched corn, and an hundred clusters of raisins, and two hundred cakes of figs, and laid them on asses.

She took all of that to provide for David's men, all 600 of them. Would that be just two bottles (skins) of alcoholic wine for all those men? No, it could only be two skins of concentrated grape syrup, which when mixed with water would have provided sufficient sweet juice for all those men.

The story of Abigail's treat for David and his men is not the only biblical story which shows the use of highly concentrated grape juice. 2Sam 16:1 tells the story of Ziba the servant of Mephibosheth, who met David on his return from a brief exile from Jerusalem. Ziba went out with a couple of asses, bearing two hundred loaves of bread, an hundred bunches of raisins, an hundred bunches of summer fruits, and a bottle of wine. That is one bottle or skin of wine for all of David's men. It had to be concentrated grape juice.

When I was invited into a French home in Africa, I was served a delicious drink where a quarter of an inch of concentrated grape syrup was poured into a glass which was then filled with water. Concentrated grape juice is abundantly used in many countries, even to the present time, and to my personal knowledge specifically in France and Italy. The bottle pictured at right and described below was listed at $19.00 a bottle!

This unique grape beverage has been produced for centuries in the Italian region of Emilia Romagna. The ancient craft of slowly cooking fresh grape juice (in Italian, Mosto d'Uva) in huge kettles and reducing it to a rich liquid is being preserved by artisans like Adriano Guerzoni and his sons. Selected grapes ... are pressed and cooked to produce a grape juice reminiscent of a sweet wine. Cooking the juice softens the sugars and concentrates the flavor. The resulting drink is rich and satisfying, with an exceptionally smooth finish.[19]

From these four arguments we can conclude from Scripture that grape juice is often mentioned in Scripture. The "truth" of the matter is clear. Grape juice is found in the Scriptural account of Israel's daily life in the Promised Land. It cannot, therefore, be true that grape juice was never mentioned in the Bible. It is also true that when the English translation says "wine," it is generic in that "wine" refers to both grape juice and an alcoholic beverage. It cannot, therefore, be true that "wine" always means an alcoholic drink.

---

[19] www.amazon.com/Guerzoni-Biodynamic-Mosto-Grape-Juice/dp/B0000U3BG0 (Accessed 3/29/11).

III. God Blesses the Natural Fruit of the Vine

Those who cannot accept that God speaks of grape juice in the Bible misunderstand a large part of the everyday life of His people in Bible times. It is clear that God talks of both grape juice and alcoholic beverages: He blesses the first and condemns the use of the second.

Let us look at what God taught His people. Before He brought them into the Promised Land, He gave them instructions which would enable them to lead a happy and prosperous life in that land. We find very specific instructions in Exodus through Deuteronomy. Just before the people entered Canaan, Moses gave the following charge in Deuteronomy 27 and 28:

> *And Moses charged the people the same day, saying, These shall stand upon mount Gerizim to bless the people, when ye are come over Jordan; ... And these shall stand upon mount Ebal to curse; And the Levites shall speak, and say unto all the men of Israel with a loud voice, Cursed be...*
>
> *If thou shalt hearken diligently unto the voice of the LORD thy God, to observe and to do all his commandments which I command thee this day, that the LORD thy God will set thee on high above all nations of the earth: And all these blessings shall come on thee...*

Israel was to divide itself in two groups and stand on two mountains which faced each other. The Levites on one mountain would utter curses against those who disobeyed God's commandments, and the Levites on the other mountain would bless specific acts of obedience to God. One act which is *not* found in the "blessings" or "cursing" lists is the blessing or cursing of grape juice or alcohol. If (as modern teaching says) grape juice does not exist in the Bible and drinking alcoholic beverages was all that God talked about, there would certainly be a problem in this place. He certainly blesses "wine" in many places in

His Word and condemns it in others. Imagine a situation in which "wine" could have been blessed from one mountain and also condemned from the other! The following illustration would affirm that what God wanted to bless was only grape juice.

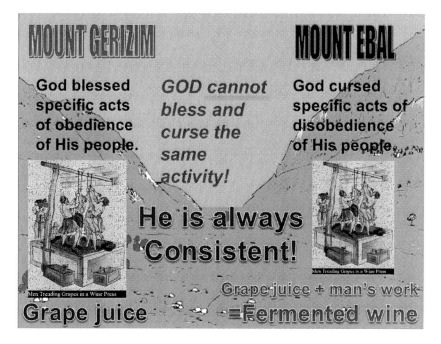

As to God's blessing grape juice, we can see from Scripture what God promised Israel: "God give thee ... plenty of corn and wine" (Genesis 27:28). When the spies came back from their visit, they carried extremely large bunches of grapes as proof that this was the land that God had promised. It is clear from Scripture that God planned for His people to have this healthy beverage (grape juice) for He mentions it 124 times in the Old Testament![20] When you drive northward out of Jerusalem, in Palestine, the mountainsides are covered with what used to be terraced vineyards. "Vine" and "vineyards" are mentioned nine times in just eight chapters in Song of Solomon! Let us get up early to the vineyards; let us see if the vine flourish, whether the tender grape appear, and the pomegranates bud forth: there will I give thee my loves

---

[20] See Robert Teachout, *op.cit.*, pp. 73, 74. He analyses each Hebrew word in the O.T. and shows its meaning, grape juice or wine.

(Song of Solomon 7:12). It is clear that vineyards and grapes were blessed by God and important to the Jews. In each vineyard there was provision for a wine press for the production of grape juice. In Scripture we find four actions of God in relation to His people which prove His blessing upon this natural product.

1. He promised His people He would provide it.

The Bible talks of "wine" as being God's blessed provision, a staple of the diet of His people even before they arrived in the Promised Land. Isaac promised Jacob: *"Therefore God give thee of the dew of heaven, and the fatness of the earth, and plenty of corn and wine"* (Gen. 27:28). Joseph promised Judah: *"The sceptre shall not depart from Judah, nor a lawgiver from between his feet, until Shiloh come; and unto him shall the gathering of the people be. Binding his foal unto the vine, and his ass's colt unto the choice vine; he washed his garments in wine, and his clothes in the blood of grapes"* (Gen. 49:10, 11). God promised through Moses: *"And he will love thee, and bless thee, and multiply thee: he will also bless the fruit of thy womb, and the fruit of thy land, thy corn, and thy wine, and thine oil, the increase of thy kine, and the flocks of thy sheep, in the land which he sware unto thy fathers to give thee"* (Deut. 7:13).

The Israelites did not always appreciate God's blessing. Later in their history God said to the prophet Hosea concerning Israel that He had given them wine: *"For she did not know that I gave her corn, and wine, and oil,..."* (Hos.2:8). He says in Psalm 104:13-15:

> *He watereth the hills from his chambers: the earth is satisfied with the fruit of thy works. He causeth the grass to grow for the cattle, and herb for the service of man: that he may bring forth food out of the earth; And wine that maketh glad the heart of man, and oil to make his face to shine, and bread which strengtheneth man's heart.*

It can be seen from all of these citations that grape juice was a basic and very important part of the diet in biblical times.

2. He *predicted* His provision for His people before the entry into the Promised Land

Did you ever wonder why the spies who brought back such a glowing report of the Promised Land also brought back bunches of grapes? God had promised this blessing to Israel. We find this in Isaac's blessing of Jacob (Gen. 27:28), *"Therefore God give thee of the dew of heaven, and the fatness of the earth, and plenty of corn and wine."* We also find this promise repeated in Deut. 11:14, *"That I will give you the rain of your land in his due season, the first rain and the latter rain, that thou mayest gather in thy corn, and thy wine, and thine oil."* Now He

wanted to encourage His people with the proof even before they arrived in their new home. Unfortunately, they could only think of the enemies (the giants) they would have to face, and the grapes would have to wait.

3. He provided it for the joy of His people

Grapes and grape juice were VERY important to people in Bible times and were easily accessible. This we know because the Bible talks much of vines and vineyards. The fresh juice was a wonderful treat.

One of the earliest references to grape juice is found in Genesis 40:11: *And Pharaoh's cup was in my hand: and I took the grapes, and pressed them into Pharaoh's cup, and I gave the cup into Pharaoh's hand.* Josephus, in his *Antiquities of the Jews*, chapter five, says: *"he squeezed them into a cup which the king held in his hand; and when he had strained the wine, he*

gave it to the king to drink. "[21] A Bible Commentary in 1810 said this:

> From this we find that wine anciently was the mere expressed juice of the grape, without fermentation. The saky, or cup-bearer, took the bunch, pressed the juice into the cup, and instantly delivered it into the hands of his master. This was anciently the yayin of the Hebrews, the oinos, of the Greeks, and the mustum of the ancient Latins.[22]

The Bible talks often of this treat of freshly squeezed grape juice as illustrated by Isaiah 65:8: *Thus saith the LORD, As the new wine is found in the cluster, ... a blessing is in it.* Albert Barnes says, "The Hebrew word (tirosh) used here means properly must, or new wine."

In a list of great blessings, God says: *"Butter of kine, and milk of sheep, with fat of lambs, and rams of the breed of Bashan, and goats, with the fat of kidneys of wheat; and thou didst drink the pure blood of the grape"* (Deuteronomy 32:14). At that time, they did not have many sources of sugar, an important element in diet. They had no candy, jam, ice cream, soft drinks, or juice drinks! The process of fermentation eliminates sugar. If "wine" in Bible times was always fermented, then wine would not provide sugar in the diet! Grapes and their juice, however, did and were a very important part of meals as well as special treats for voyages.

---

[21] Josephus, *Antiquities of the Jews*, Book 2, Chapter 5.

[22] Adam Clarke *Commentary, Genesis 40:11.* http://www.studylight.org/com/acc/ view.cgi? book=ge&chapter=040. (Accessed 7/22/2011).

4. He proclaimed the use of it for the fellowship of His people

In the Old Testament God constantly encourages the *importance* and *wellbeing* of the family. A strong, healthy family was the result of the practice of the Jewish faith. One of the important parts of that practice was the system of feasts established by God where the families were to unite regularly at home, at the tabernacle, or at the temple to fellowship with God and with each other. In these feast times, "wine" is said to have played a large part. God gave instructions for those who lived close to the temple and for those who lived far away, both of whom were required to present themselves before the Lord. For those who lived nearby:

> *And thou shalt eat before the LORD thy God, in the place which he shall choose to place his name there, the tithe of thy corn, of thy wine, and of thine oil, and the firstlings of thy herds and of thy flocks; that thou mayest learn to fear the LORD thy God always (De 14:23).*

For those who lived far away, they were to sell their produce in their homes and bring the money to the temple:

> *And thou shalt bestow that money for whatsoever thy soul lusteth after, for oxen, or for sheep, or for wine, or for strong drink, or for whatsoever thy soul desireth: and thou shalt eat there before the LORD thy God, and thou shalt rejoice, thou, and thine household, (De 14:26).*

If this "wine" was not grape juice, there is a problem of consistency in the instructions for sacrifices and feasts. Not only are there instances where priests are commanded to both drink and not drink "wine," but Israel was told to bring both "wine" and strong drink as an offering to the Lord. Numbers 15:7 says: *And for a drink offering thou shalt offer the third part of an hin of wine, for a sweet savour unto the LORD.* The Bible goes on to speak several times of wine used as an offering. Since

God spoke so often about "no leaven" in His offerings, it seems unreasonable to believe He would permit it for His drink offerings.

It is clear that God can only bless natural grape juice. In His Word He reveals the importance of this healthy drink by promising it to His people and by providing it for their enjoyment during times of worship and socializing.

IV.   God's Problem with Alcohol

Throughout the Old Testament we read how God blesses grape juice in the Bible. However, in the Scriptures God clearly reveals that He has a major problem with alcohol. He very specifically talks about its effects on the human body. It is easy to see in Scripture that there is a world of difference between the natural juice of a natural fruit and man-made alcohol that is made by adding something to the juice which changes it completely.

In 1919 Richmond Pearson Hobson published a book, *Alcohol and the Human Race*. He, as a member of Congress, was urged by his political advisors to vote against a Prohibition amendment. He resisted the tremendous pressure that was building against the Prohibition movement and decided to study all that was available in the Library of Congress. This is what he said about his findings:

> *"I was startled to find, almost at the outset, that alcohol is not a product built up of grain, grapes and other food materials, but is the toxin of yeast or ferment germs, which, after devouring the food materials, excrete alcohol as their waste product."[23]*

We must never forget that in all discussion of wine in the Bible, if it is a fermented drink it is NOT a natural drink. It is a man-made, poisonous product. Let's examine two things Christians often say today about wine: *1. "If you wait just a little bit, grape juice turns to wine."* *2."Since God made wine, then it is good for us. Let us partake!"*

Nothing could be further from the truth than to think that grape juice turns to wine automatically. Making wine is a *process* which was discovered centuries ago. Wikipedia gives this summary of wine-making:

> *To start primary fermentation yeast is added to the must for red wine or juice for white wine. During this fermentation, which*

---

[23] Richmond Pearson Hobson, *Alcohol and the Human Race*, 1919, p. 7. (Published by Google Books).

often takes between one and two weeks, the yeast converts most of the sugars in the grape juice into ethanol (alcohol) and carbon dioxide. The carbon dioxide is lost to the atmosphere. After the primary fermentation of red grapes the free run wine is pumped off into tanks and the skins are pressed to extract the remaining juice and wine, the press wine blended with the free run wine at the wine makers discretion. The wine is kept warm and the remaining sugars are converted into alcohol and carbon dioxide. The next process in the making of red wine is secondary fermentation. This is a bacterial fermentation which converts malic acid to lactic acid. This process decreases the acid in the wine and softens the taste of the wine. Red wine is sometimes transferred to oak barrels to mature for a period of weeks or months, this practice imparts oak aromas to the wine. The wine must be settled or clarified and adjustments made prior to filtration and bottling.[24]

Grape juice which is not treated, i.e. either boiled to concentrate the sugar content or fermented to make alcohol, will simply spoil and smell. However, treating grape juice to preserve it as grape juice was and is relatively easy. Much is written in Roman and Greek writings about the use of preserved grape juice:

Defrutum, carenum, *and* **sapa** *were reductions of must used in Roman cuisine. They were made by boiling down grape juice or must (freshly squeezed grapes) in large kettles until it had been reduced to two-thirds the original volume, carenum; half the original volume, defrutum; and one-third, sapa. The main culinary use of defrutum was to help preserve and sweeten wine, but it was also added to fruit and meat dishes as a sweetening and souring agent and even given to food animals such as suckling pig and duck to improve the taste of their flesh.[25]*

[24] "Wine-making," *Wikipedia.* http://en.wikipedia.org/wiki/Winemaking (Accessed 12/06/2010).
[25] http://en.wikipedia.org/wiki/Defrutum (Accessed 8/5/2011).

This and other historical references to boiled "must" simply show that it was *available* in Bible times and was easily preserved as concentrated, non-alcoholic grape juice.

God did not make wine. He made grape juice and man created wine. William Patton cites many authorities of his time concerning this. I will quote two:

> *Sir Humphrey Davy says of alcohol: "It has never been found ready formed in plants." Count Chaptal, the eminent French chemist, says: "Nature never made spirituous liquors: she rots the grape upon the branch, but it is _art_ which converts the juice into (alcoholic) wine.*[26]

Instead of being a God-given, pure, natural juice, wine is a poisonous product made by man. God has much to say about its effects upon the human body.

God clearly condemns "wine" in Scripture:

> *Wine is a mocker, strong drink is raging; and whosoever is deceived thereby is not wise (Proverbs 20:1).*

> *Who hath woe? who hath sorrow? who hath contentions? who hath babbling? who hath wounds without cause? who hath redness of eyes? They that tarry long at the wine… (Proverbs 23:29,30).*

> *They grope in the dark without light, and he maketh them to stagger like a drunken man (Job 12:25).*

> *Woe unto them that are mighty to drink wine…(Isaiah 5:22)*

> *Woe unto them that rise up early in the morning, that they may follow strong drink; that continue until night, till wine inflame them! (Isaiah 5:11).*

---

[26] Patton, William, *Bible Wines or The Laws of Fermentation and Wines of the Ancients.* New York:National Temperance Society and Publication House, 1871, p. 92.

> *Let us walk honestly, as in the day; not in rioting and drunkenness;... (Romans 13:13).*

> *And be not drunk with wine, wherein is excess.... (Ephesians 5:18).*

> *Look not thou upon the wine when it is red, when it giveth his colour in the cup, when it moveth itself aright (Proverbs 23:31).*

God commands the priests not to drink wine:

> *Do not drink wine nor strong drink, thou, nor thy sons with thee, when ye go into the tabernacle of the congregation, lest ye die: (Leviticus 10:9).*

God describes wine as poison:

> *Their wine is the poison of dragons, and the cruel venom of asps (Deuteronomy 32:33).*

God talks of those who were "drunken" and what they did: Noah did that which was wrong because he was under the influence of alcohol:

> *And he drank of the wine, and was drunken... (Gen 9:21).*

Lot drank and sinned:

> *And they made their father drink wine that night: and the firstborn went in, and lay with her father; and he perceived not when she lay down, nor when she arose (Genesis 19:33).*

Eli was used to seeing people under the influence:

> *And Eli said unto her, How long wilt thou be drunken? put away thy wine from thee (1Samuel 1:14).*

Nabal's drinking cost him his life and so did Amnon's:

*Nabal's heart was merry within him, for he was very drunken...
(1Samuel 25:36).*

*Mark ye now when Amnon's heart is merry with wine... (2Samuel
13:28).*

Ahasuerus tried to subject his queen to public humiliation because he
had drunk too much alcohol. He would never have done this while
sober, for in their culture one did not parade one's wife before other
men!

*And they gave them drink in vessels of gold, ... and royal wine in
abundance.... On the seventh day, when the heart of the king was
merry with wine, he commanded.... to bring Vashti the queen
before the king with the crown royal, to shew the people and the
princes her beauty: for she was fair to look on. (Esther 1:7,10,11).*

God characterizes wine as promoting violence:

*For they eat the bread of wickedness, and drink the wine of
violence (Proverbs 4:17).*

In summarizing the teaching from all the passages in the Bible, we find
that God severely condemns alcoholic beverages for His people for the
following reasons:

- ✓ *it keeps one who drinks from drawing near to God;*
- ✓ *it deceives one who drinks--The very first drink goes directly
  to the brain and reduces a person's resistance to sin;*
- ✓ *it inflames one who drinks;*
- ✓ *it causes one who drinks to err and to stumble;*
- ✓ *it causes one who drinks to stagger;*
- ✓ *it causes one who drinks to be poor;*
- ✓ *it causes one who drinks to sin;*
- ✓ *it causes one who drinks to be violent.*

God's problem with alcoholic wine is that men made it and drank it.
His solution seems pretty simple: don't drink it. When people speak to

me and say, "… but wine in the Bible was highly diluted and was not nearly as alcoholic as now…" I simply answer, "But in the Bible, people got drunk when they drank it!" God warns where that leads.

V.   Preserving Grape Juice in Bible Times

Although we have seen from many Scriptures that grape juice was indeed spoken of in the Bible, we must consider the number one proof advanced by all those who insist that "wine" in the Bible is ALWAYS intoxicating. This "proof" is simple: they maintain that since there was no refrigeration in ancient times, there could be no preservation of natural grape juice.

To show how easily grape juice was made in biblical times, I will cite first of all from a story I found recently on the Internet.

A French family was traveling around the world, putting their experiences on the Internet, with pictures. They arrived in the highest town in the mountains of central Turkey. (I will translate and shorten their story and include some of the pictures they took).[27]

> *We were continuing our route when an irresistible call stopped us. We had seen a small family busy in front of their dwelling. They saw us and motioned us to approach. We watched them and took pictures, and then they gave us a detailed recipe for making concentrated grape juice:*

> 1. *Put good bunches of white grapes in two or three rice sacks.*
>
> 2. *Put on boots and trample the raisins to let the juice go into a basin, then filter.*

---

[27] http://www.aventureuse-balade.net/reportages/raisin.html (Accessed: 8/5/2009). With permission.

3. Put the juice in a large pot on a wood fire and bring to a boil.

4. Strain the foam. Let it boil. Strain off the foam again.

Treading grapes

5. Put the boiling juice in a large plastic container and let it "rest" all night.

6. Put it back on the fire and continue #4 until the juice turns brown.

Collecting juice

7. Taste it – it's delicious!

This story and this "recipe" are given by those who observed people who live in our present time and who were using a simple way of making concentrated grape juice syrup, a method which goes back to Bible times.

Boiling

Tasting

It is interesting to note what John George Marshall wrote in 1855 in a book about "wine" in the Bible in which he detailed proof for the preservation of grape juice in Bible times:

Several modes were known in the vine countries of the East, and were very generally practiced, for preserving the "fruit," or liquid of the grape, from fermentation; and keeping it in that state, sweet, and free from the intoxicating quality, for any

*time desired. The chief mode it appears, [was], -- boiling
down the juice of the grape to syrup....*[28]

Marshall also cites a celebrated oriental traveler that he met in
Edinburgh who "stated that the Mahometans (Muslims) to
whom intoxicating drink of any kind is forbidden, carried
with them in their journeys the unfermented wine."[29] We can
add that the Koran clearly outlaws alcoholic wine for all
Muslims and yet blesses grapes and their production, which
obviously shows that they could preserve it. Here are two
interesting quotes from a Muslim source on the Internet:

> *6.99 It is He Who* sendeth *down rain from the skies: with it We
> produce vegetation of all kinds: from some We produce green
> (crops), out of which We produce grain, heaped up (at
> harvest); out of the date-palm and its sheaths (or spathes)
> (come) clusters of dates hanging low and near: and (then
> there are) gardens of grapes, and olives, and pomegranates,
> each similar (in kind) yet different (in variety): when they
> begin to bear fruit, feast your eyes with the fruit and the
> ripeness thereof.*

> *We all know that wine is forbidden in this world and that it causes
> intoxication and fogs the mind; hence it is rijs (an abomination)
> and the handiwork of the Shaytaan, and it is the mother of all
> evils as the Prophet (blessings and peace of Allaah be upon
> him). My question is: why is wine haraam (prohibited) in
> this world and halaal (permissible) in the hereafter The
> answer that is given is very interesting: Allaah describes the
> wine of the hereafter as: pure white wine; delicious to the
> drinkers, unlike the wine of this world which is distasteful when*

---

[28] *The "Strong Drink" Delusion, with its Criminal and Ruinous Results Exposed*, by John George
Marshall, the Journal Office, Halifax, 1855. The author goes on to cite other methods and ancient
writers who discuss this.

[29] Marshall, p. 23.

38

drunk; having no "ghoul" (hurt, abdominal pain, headache) – in short, fresh grape juice.[30]

In the first chapter, I told of experiencing first-hand another way of preserving grape juice which also goes back to Bible times. In fact there are many modern authors who document a great many ancient methods of preservation. The easiest was to keep the juice fresh by simply bringing it to a boil and then sealing it in a bottle or jug and keeping it in a cellar or cave. Also, they could boil the syrup to a paste which was easy to carry. Of course, they could also preserve the grapes whole in order to make their juice later in the year.[31] This is discussed at length in Appendix I.

---

[30] Question and answer about wine on a Muslim Internet site. The answer was given: that which Allah will give in hereafter is pure and not fermented. http://www.islamqa.com/en/ref/127938. (accessed: 8/5/2009).
[31] Pliny, ancient Roman nobleman, scientist and historian, author of, *Pliny's Natural History* said: Some grapes will last all through the winter if the clusters are hung by a string from the ceiling... Cited by Jim McGuiggan, The Bible, the Saint, & the Liquor Industry, 1977, p.64.

VI. A Historical Problem with Alcohol: A Quick Look at the Battle for Temperance

We cannot properly understand the present bias against finding grape juice in the Bible or the actual tidal wave of Christians beginning to drink alcohol without looking back in history to a time when this interpretational and practical battle was fought on a massive scale. That whole era is often called "Prohibition." It included the battle for temperance as well as the actual time when Prohibition was the law of the land.

Today, the popular claim from both sides of the issue is that the law that banned the sale and production of alcoholic beverages was a failure. The following quote follows the accepted analysis of today:

> *National prohibition of alcohol (1920-33)--the "noble experiment"--was undertaken to reduce crime and corruption, solve social problems, reduce the tax burden created by prisons and poorhouses, and improve health and hygiene in America. The results of that experiment clearly indicate that it was a miserable failure on all counts.[32]*

However, this is a very short-sighted view. Not only did Prohibition have a beneficial effect on society as a whole, but the Christian Bible teaching which greatly helped to produce it had an effect on Christianity that would last a hundred years. This will be shown in the next chapter.

Concerning the state of society before Prohibition, a historian said, in a book written in 1920:

> *At the opening of the century it really seemed as if the manhood of America was about to be drowned in strong drink. The cheapness of untaxed intoxicants— rum, whiskey, and apple-jack, made by anyone who chose to undertake the business and sold at every*

---

[32] Cato Institute Policy Analysis, http://www.cato.org/pub_display.php?pub_id=1017, (Accessed 7/22/2011).

gathering of the people without reference to the age or sex of the purchaser—had made drunkenness almost universal. Samuel Brech, writing at the close of the eighteenth century, says that "it was impossible to secure a servant— white or black, bond or free—who could be depended on to keep sober for twenty-four hours. All classes and professions were affected. The judge was overcome on the bench; the minister sometimes staggered on his way to the pulpit..." [33]

Rev. Lyman Beecher, who was describing the ordination of a minister at Plymouth, Connecticut, in 1810, said:

At this ordination the preparation for our creature comforts besides food included a broad sideboard covered with decanters and bottles.... The drinking was apparently universal... they always took something to drink around, also before public services, and always on their return. [34]

Not only was society going down the slippery slope of more and more consumption of alcohol, but many Christians followed right along. This being the state of the church and Christianity, it is a great wonder that Prohibition happened at all and that it *accomplished* anything.

An adequate history of the battles for abstinence cannot be undertaken here. In a survey, the epoch will be summarized with cameos of some of the preachers of the time who worked very hard to teach God's Word on the subject as well as some preachers and writers who opposed them.

---

[33] Thompson, *The Hand of God in American History*, p. 559, cited in Milner, Duncan C., *Lincoln and Liquor*, The Neale Publishing Company, 440 Fourth Avenue, New York, 1920, p.13.

[34] Milner, Duncan C., *Lincoln and Liquor*, The Neale Publishing Company, 440 Fourth Avenue, New York, 1920, p. 15.

Preachers who espoused the cause of abstinence

Though it is possible to find many writings from those who sought to inform Christians of what the Bible says about "wine," we will look at just a few who led the tremendous effort. Lumpkins gives a list of eminent scholars of the 19th century who believed there was both fermented and unfermented "wine" in the Bible:

> *Adam Clarke, Albert Barnes, Thomas Scott, Ralph Wardlaw, F.R. Lees, James Smith, George Duffield, Dawson Burns, Taylor Lewis, William Patton, G. W. Samson, Moses Stewart, Canon F.W. Farrar, Alonzo Potter, G. Bush, and Norman Kerr.*[35]

The availability of writings from the early 1800's has been greatly helped by the fact that Google has put many of them on the internet in Google Books.

Lyman Beecher: the Cofounder of the American Temperance Society.

Lyman Beecher was a Presbyterian pastor in Boston in the early 1800's. By 1826 when he began preaching on intemperance, he was known as one of the foremost preachers of his day and his efforts resulted in a significant spiritual awakening. He had a reputation for defending orthodoxy. His messages on alcohol were not particularly appreciated in Boston. In fact he knew several setbacks, but always persevered.

> *Even in 1812, when Lyman Beecher proposed to his fellow Congregational ministers that they formulate a program for combating intemperance, ... "the regular committee reported that 'after faithful and prayerful inquiry' it was convinced that nothing could be done to check the growth of intemperance."*[36]

To the contrary, his messages and his work did produce results. He co-founded the American Temperance Society in 1826, and that society

---

[35] Lumpkins, *op. cit.,* p. 119.
[36] http://aa-nia-dist11.org/Documents/roots2.pdf (Accessed 12/13/2010).

grew quickly. His *"Six Sermons on Intemperance,"* given in 1828, were powerful support for temperance. His message was simple.

Intemperance is the sin of our land, and if anything shall defeat the hopes of the world, which hang upon our experiment of civil liberty, it is that river of fire [intemperance], which is rolling through the land, destroying the vital air, and extending around an atmosphere of death.[37]

This message was sorely needed.

Temperance activism arose at a time when the consumption of distilled liquor was at an all-time high. In 1810, whiskey and other distilled liquors constituted the country's third most important industrial product, and distilling was a notable economic activity on the frontier because of the high costs of shipping grain.[38]

Within five years there were 2,220 local chapters in the U.S. with 170,000 members who had taken a pledge to abstain from drinking distilled beverages.[39] He later moved from Boston to Cincinnati where he continued his preaching on the subject.

George Marshall: Noted Jurist and Converted Alcoholic.

George Marshall was a Canadian judge in Nova Scotia. In 1823 he was named chief justice of the Inferior Court of Common Pleas. He also served as president of the Courts of General and Special Sessions and justice of the peace for Cape Breton. He was well known and wrote a definitive work on Canadian Law. In 1824, after a significant time of soul-searching and searching the Scriptures, he accepted the Lord as his personal Savior. He stopped all "partaking" of alcoholic beverages in 1824. He visited Boston in 1831 and read Lyman Beecher's sermons.

---

[37] http://utc.iath.virginia.edu/sentimnt/sneslbat.html. {Accessed 7/5/2011).
[38] *Ibid.*
[39] Wikipedia, http://en.wikipedia.org/wiki/American_Temperance_Society. (Accessed 12/11/2010).

In 1842, he retired as a judge and started traveling and speaking against alcohol across Canada, in the United States, and in Great Britain. In 1855 he wrote *Strong Drink Delusion, with its Criminal and Ruinous Results Exposed*. In this book he documented the case for grape juice in the Bible both from Scripture and from ancient writings. In a book written in 1866, he details a great many of the crimes he had encountered while on the bench and the influence of alcohol in those crimes.[40]

Eliphalet Nott: Noted Pastor, Scientist, Inventor, College President

Eliphalet Nott was one of the most respected pastors, scholars, and lecturers of his time. He was also a scientist with several noted inventions, including the first anthracite coal stove, which was named for him. In 1798, he became pastor of the First Presbyterian Church of Albany, New York, which included a number of prestigious political leaders in the congregation.

In 1800 he was named co-chaplain of the New York State legislature and a trustee of Union College in Schenectady. In 1804 he was named president of that college which was the third largest in America, behind Yale and Harvard. Under Nott's presidency, Union College flourished and graduated the largest class in the United States at that time. His most famous series of lectures was "*Lectures on Temperance*" published in 1847. He was a fiery advocate of abstinence and regularly declared that the Bible could not be used to defend moderate drinking:

> *In the preceding lectures, we have shown that a kind of wine has existed from great antiquity, which was injurious to health and subversive of morals; that these evils, since the introduction of distillation, have been greatly increased; that half the lunacy, three-fourths of the pauperism, and five-sixths of the crime with which the nation is visited, is owing to intemperance; that there are believed to be five hundred thousand drunkards in the*

---

[40] *Personal Narratives with Reflections and Remarks*, Halifax, N.S. T Chamberlain, 176 Argyle St 1866, Harvard College, Google e-books.

*republic, and that thousands die of drunkenness annually. We
have also shown that drunkenness results from moderate drinking,
and that drunkenness must continue, by a necessity of nature, as
long as habitual temperate drinking is continued;...*

*...they who so use intoxicating liquors violate an established law
of nature, and drunkenness, disease and death, which result from
such use, are the penalty which follows, by the appointment of
God, the violation of that law; that God wills the happiness of his
creatures, and when the authority of the Bible, is plead in behalf
of any usage that leads to misery, it may be known that the Bible
is plead in error in behalf of such usage; that in the present
instance, and so far as the wines of commerce are concerned, to
appeal to the Bible as authority, is absurd; that the Bible knows
nothing and teaches nothing directly, in relation to these wines of
commerce- the same being either a brandied or drugged article,
never in use in Palestine; that in relation to these spurious articles
the book of nature must alone be consulted, and that being
consulted, their condemnation will be found on many a page,
inscribed in characters of wrath...*[41]

I have read many statements that are frankly contemptuous of those
who wrote in the early 1800's. It is disgraceful that we should dismiss
their findings so easily when they were very godly men who studied
the subject meticulously. It should be noted that there were a great
many such men.

Opposition to abstinence

In the battle for abstinence it is not to be thought that those who so ably
espoused abstinence from a biblical standpoint did not face vigorous
opposition from those who denigrated their position. Most of the clergy
in denominations that were turning liberal partook freely of alcoholic

---

[41] *Lectures on Temperance* by Eliphalet Nott (no XI).

beverages and were firmly opposed to any thought that the Bible did NOT condone moderate drinking. This opposition was very vocal.

One of the most vocal was Howard Crosby, pastor of Fourth Avenue Presbyterian Church, New York City, and Chancellor of New York University beginning in 1870. When invited to speak in the pulpit of a noted proponent of total abstinence, he gave a discourse which he entitled "*Calm View of the Temperance Question.*" In his address, he asserts that the total-abstinence system is contrary to revealed religion and harmful to the interests of the country, exclaiming:

> *I charge upon this system [total abstinence] the growth of drunkenness in our land and the general demoralization among religious communities; and I call upon all sound-minded thinking men to stop the enormities of this false system.*[42]

Later he wrote:

> *There is not a chemist or a classical scholar in the world who would dare risk his reputation on the assertion that there was ever an unfermented wine in common use [in Bible times], knowing well, that "must" preserved from fermentation is called wine only by a kind of courtesy... and that this could never, in the nature of things be a common drink.*[43]

> *Prof. Burnstead makes similar assertions; declaring that the "theory" of an unfermented wine has failed to commend itself to the scholarship of the world.*[44]

Dr. Moore, a contemporary of Dr Crosby, remarked, "The history of the doctrine of unfermented Bible wine cannot be carried back beyond a few decades; and this fact furnishes a préjugé légitime against it (a legitimate prejudice)."[45] He is saying that the lack of longevity of the

---

[42] http://books.google.com/books?id=7tYXAAAAYAAJ&pg=PA89&lpg=PA109&ots=N9e050ey eN&dq=chancellor+crosby&output=text#c_top (Accessed 7/7/2011).

[43] Field, Leon C., *Oinos: A Discussion of the Bible Wine Question,* Phillips & Hunt, NY, NY, 1883; p.17.

[44] Ibid

[45] Ibid

"unfermented Bible wine" doctrine is a sufficient reason for not believing that theory. This can also be seen in another quote from an author in 1883:

> *At the opening of the present year, (1881) and almost simultaneously, Chancellor Crosby on the platform of the Monday Lectureship, Dr. Moore in the pages of the "Presbyterian Review," and Prof. Burnstead in the pages of the " Bibliotheca Sacra," made vigorous onslaught on those who hold that the Bible does not lend its sanction to the use of intoxicating beverages, and, in particular, on all who quote the example of Christ in favor of total abstinence. "No unbiased reader," Chancellor Crosby declares, "can for a moment doubt that wine as referred to in the Bible (passim) is an intoxicating drink, and that such wine was drunk by our Savior and the early Christians."* [46]

Chancellor Crosby was a spirited and contemptuous foe of the temperance movement. He said that there is a class of biblical scholars and interpreters "who do assert that wherever wine is referred to in the Bible with approbation it is unfermented wine." Of this class of men, Dr. Crosby says:

> ... *"their learned ignorance is splendid "; they are " inventors of a theory of magnificent daring"; they " use false texts" and "deceptive arguments"; "deal dishonestly with the Scriptures"; "beg the question and build on air"; their theory is a "fable," born of "falsehoods," supported by " Scripture-twisting and wriggling"; their arguments are "cobwebs," and their zeal outstrips their judgment, and they plan to "undermine the Bible".* [47]

---

[46] Ibid, p. 1

[47] Review of Dr. Crosby's *Calm view of temperance*, http://books.google.com/books (Accessed 7/28/2011).

More than one hundred years later, many modern writers and speakers who promote moderate drinking also seem to convey the thought that grape juice in the Bible is a fairly new idea in the Christian community and is promoted by unworthy and dishonest writers. Nothing could be further from the truth. The dates and the quotes already furnished in this chapter prove that very proficient and respected students of God's word taught, preached, and wrote about grape juice in the Bible in preceding centuries.

It is interesting to compare those who espoused the cause of abstinence with those of the 1800's who opposed them. On the one hand there was scholarship, searching ancient texts and studying the biblical references to try to understand the text. On the other hand it is observed that there was character assassination of and ridicule toward those who found grape juice in the Bible. Those who reject grape juice in the Bible today do not have a very flattering opinion of those who accept this truth; historically, that has always been the case.

48

VII.   Can we KNOW what *IS* true?

The title of this book could very well have been: is *Grape Juice is in the Bible: TRUE or FALSE?*, for the task of this study is to determine "what is the TRUTH of the matter." Unfortunately, we are living in an era when, even among theologians, there is considerable debate as to whether or not objective truth exists and if it is possible to know what truth is.

That there should be such a debate is sad! To say that the creator of the universe does not know what truth is or how to reveal it is sheer unbelief in the God of the Bible. Can God speak anything but the truth?

> *Truth is defined as that which conforms to reality. Not reality as people think they see it, but reality as it actually exists - as only God sees it. For the God- breathed Scriptures to be anything less than the truth, God must have made a mistake or lied.*[48]

Truth is certainly important to God. He uses words like *truth* and *true* and *truly* almost 400 times in the Bible.

> *The Scriptures repeatedly associate what is true and truth with God. The primary Old Testament word used for this association is "emet" (Hebrew). Its foundational concept is "certainty, dependability"; and it is used "in several categories of contexts, all of which relate to God directly or indirectly."*[49]

From this and many Scripture passages, it can be affirmed that:

- Biblical Truth is absolute, never relative.
- Biblical Truth is objective, never subjective.
- Biblical Truth is what corresponds to reality.

---

[48] Emmons, *His Word is Truth*, Israel My Glory, Jan/Feb 2009
[49] Renald Showers *The Foundations of Faith: God is True and Truth* http://www.foi.org/ godistrueandtruth . (Accessed 7/28/2011).

God's Word says in Deuteronomy 32:4: "*He is the Rock, his work is perfect: for all his ways are judgment: a God of truth and without iniquity, just and right is he.*" David says, "*Lead me in thy truth, and teach me: for thou art the God of my salvation; on thee do I wait all the day*" (Ps 25:5). Jesus said, "*I am the truth.*"

In today's culture, the increasingly-popular idea of truth makes it subject to human experience. This idea simply rejects the plain sense of Scripture. The truth of Scripture is objective, not subjective, and is never affected by the interpreter's understanding.

It is a fact that Christians in America are less and less interested in "objective truth." In fact, there has been a massive swing away from truth as truth, as affirmed by the results of a poll published by *World Magazine*, Aug. 2008, pp. 4 and 26:

- *63% of Americans don't think that truth is knowable.*
- *53% of those who call themselves evangelical Christians are similarly skeptical.*
- *Most Americans agree that there are clear and absolute standards for what is right and wrong. But a little more than half rely on "practical experience and common sense." Only 29 % say that their religion is their guide for determining those standards.*

Raymond Teachout, a Baptist missionary in Quebec, has written a book, *Adrift from the Gospel,* which speaks much about "truth." He says in discussing the "interpretation barrier":

Few Evangelicals put in question the fact that God has given us His revelation.

However, what is often put in question is the clarity and perspicuity of Scripture. "Yes," they would say, "truth has been given. But it is beyond us to ever come to a sure interpretation of that revealed truth." Thus, truth is thereby made inaccessible; we can only attain to "truth."

Consider this quote from JOHN STOTT. He says in his popular book, Evangelical Truth:

> *In particular, we need a greater measure of discernment, so that we may distinguish between evangelical essentials which cannot be compromised and those adiaphora (matters indifferent) on which being of secondary importance it is not necessary for us to insist. Perhaps our criterion for deciding which is which, a truly evangelical principle because it concerns the supremacy of Scripture, should be as follows. Whenever equally biblical Christians, who are equally anxious to understand the teaching of Scripture and to submit to its authority, reach different conclusions, we should deduce that evidently Scripture is not crystal clear in this matter, and therefore we can afford to give one another liberty.* [50]

Teachout goes on to say: *"In calling into question the clarity and/or sufficiency of Scripture, it is impossible to come to a sure interpretation of Scripture."* [51]

In other words, IF one does not accept the clarity and/or sufficiency of Scripture, one CANNOT understand Scripture. It must be added here that the fact that God's REVELATION is clear – meant to be understood – is one of the basic rules of biblical Interpretation which goes back to the time of the Reformation and which will be discussed in the next chapter.

In the search for the truth concerning grape juice, the thesis that the Word of God is not clear and is therefore open to diverse ways of interpreting a given Scripture would make it impossible to know the truth. Yet the Bible, in Jesus' own words, says: *"And ye shall know the truth, and the truth shall make you free"* (John 8:32). It is obvious that

---

[50] Teachout, Raymond L., *Adrift from the Gospel*, (Chateau-Richer,QCE, EBA, 2011), p. 149. His quote from Stott is from John Stott, *Evangelical Truth* (Downers Grove, IL.: InterVarsity Press, 1999), pp. 116-117.

[51] *Ibid*

if God's truth does not express reality, it will certainly not make us free. This same confident assurance that one can know the truth is found in many other passages in the Bible.

There follows a quote from *Adrift from the Gospel* which will help us in the study of the principles of interpretation of the Bible in the next chapter. This discussion illustrates the fact that in the Bible the truth has been revealed, the truth is understandable, and the solution to understanding Scriptural truth is humility and faithfulness.[52]

A. The Truth has been Revealed (Jn 18:38; Heb. 11:1, 6-7)

The story of Noah will serve as model. The reality of judgment (the flood) was revealed by God to Noah who believed the revelation and acted upon it. Noah made known this revelation as a preacher of righteousness (2 Peter 2:5), but no one but his family would believe. People preferred thinking that there would not be a flood and they perished in stupor.

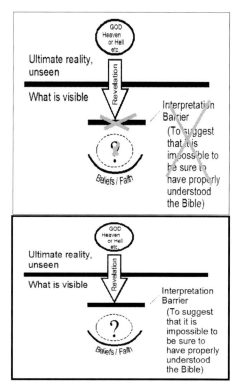

For us also, without revelation, we would be blocked, unable to know what is the ultimate reality and end of all things, and we would perish in our sins.

However, God has revealed the truth (Heb. 1:1; 2:1-3; 2 Tim. 3:15-17; Ps. 19; Rom. 1:18-19). Like Noah, it is both possible *and* necessary

---

[52] The material under the headings A, B, and C are taken directly from Teachout, Raymond L., *Adrift from the Gospel*, EBPA, pages 224-227 with the permission of the author. It is reproduced without italics.

that we align our beliefs and faith with what God reveals as to the ultimate reality of things. By faith, it is necessary to accept the revealed warning of judgment and offer of salvation in Jesus-Christ.

B. The Truth is Understandable

Not only did God reveal truth but He revealed it in a way for it to be understood.   In   fact,   God made   the   truth   under- standable   to   the   point   of making man accountable to that revelation.   Man is without   excuse   because God has made known the truth (c.f. John 12:47-48).

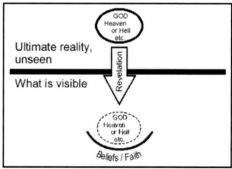

Paul's   epistle   to   Titus develops the subject of the importance of truth.   That is why Paul exhorts Titus to proclaim with authority the Word of God (Tit. 1:9; 2:15).

Unfortunately, some would argue that we have no real basis of truly knowing because we cannot be sure to have properly understood God's revelation. An interpretation barrier of some sort is set up, barring us from the certainty of knowing the truth (i.e. we are only able to *think* we know the truth; we are confined to the realm of opinions...). This is sometimes what motivates people to be inclusive in their outlook.

What does the Bible say regarding the problem of interpretation? 2Peter 3:14-16 mentions that some parts of Scripture are hard to understand, but in saying "hard" it does not mean impossible. If even the hard parts of Scripture are able to be understood, how much more the parts that define fundamentally what is a true Christian? In fact, Peter warns in that passage about those who twist the meaning of Scripture unto their own ruin.

In <u>Mark 12:24</u>, Christ's reaction to those who questioned him was not: "Oh, I see how the Bible was not clear on that subject..." (God forbid!). It was rather: "*Do ye not therefore err, because ye know not the scriptures, neither the power of God?*"

Man gets all the blame for misunderstanding the Bible, for the Bible, in itself is clear in what it reveals. Man's deceitful heart is the source of the problem. There is no such thing as an interpretation barrier.

C. Solution: Humility and Faithfulness

The proper response to God's model of revelation is not flippant and superficial dictatorial arrogance (as we sometimes sadly see), but a serious study of God's Word in order to be able to be found as "*workman that needeth not to be ashamed, rightly dividing the Word of God*" (2Tim. 2:15). 1Thessalonians 5:21-22 says: "*Prove all things, hold fast that which is good.*"

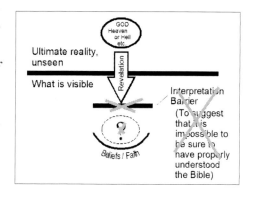

We must proclaim what God says faithfully, without adding to it, or taking away from it (Prov. 30:5-6; 2 Tim. 4:1-2; Titus 2:1, 15).

The unsaved will be judged according to the Word of God at the great white throne (Rev. 20:11-15; John 12:48; Rom. 2:16). Christians will give account unto God at Christ's judgment seat (2 Cor. 4:5; 5:10). Those who preach and teach God's Word will be judged more severely (James 3:1). It is not because no one will be perfectly faithful that one should not strive for that faithfulness God desires of us. (Here ends Teachout's quote).

It is certain that if the ancient Words from God in the Bible do not express truth, then they are not from God and can do nothing for us.

54

But they do express truth -- truth that is knowable, understandable, absolute, objective, and which corresponds to reality. Truth, according to the Theological Dictionary of the New Testament, *"is used absolutely to denote a reality which is to be regarded as amen 'firm,' and therefore 'solid,' 'valid,' or 'binding.'"*[53] In the present study, it will be found that the truth of the matter is that there is indeed grape juice in the Bible. This truth will then help us to know what God wants us to do as Christians about alcoholic consumption.

---

[53] Gottfried Quell, "emet," *Theological Dictionary of the New Testament*, ed. Gerhard Kittel (Grand Rapids: Eerdmans, 1964), 1:232.

VIII.   Rightly Dividing the Word of Truth

As I was researching *"On the fruit of the vine...,"* I had an interview with one of the leading opponents of the "grape juice in the Bible" position. He has a PHD and teaches, among other subjects, Biblical Hermeneutics. which is the study of the theory and practice of the interpretation of the Bible. He kept saying that there was no mention of grape juice in the Bible, and I kept citing verses to show that there was mention of grape juice. Finally, he said: "It is simply a matter of hermeneutics". I agreed with him immediately on that statement, though I disagree strongly with his interpretation.

God's Word is a written revelation, His perfect and complete communication to man. Let's look at what He says:

> *O LORD, thou art my God; I will exalt thee, I will praise thy name; for thou hast done wonderful things; thy counsels of old are faithfulness and <u>truth</u> (Isa 25:1).*

> *For the word of the LORD is right; and all his works are done in <u>truth</u> (Ps 33:4).*

> *For the LORD is good; his mercy is everlasting; and his <u>truth</u> endureth to all generations (Ps 100:5).*

In these verses and others in the Bible, we find that God communicated with all generations, not just with those who originally received the revelation. Remember: *"whatsoever things were written aforetime were written for our learning."* We also find that truth is important to God. In Exodus 34, where God is revealing Himself to Moses, He says this: *"The LORD, The LORD God, merciful and gracious, longsuffering, and abundant in goodness and truth"* (v. 6.). In one of his most important pronouncements Jesus said, *"I am the way, the truth, and the life."*

What is truth? Pilate asked that question of Jesus, and it is still an important question today, because in every strata of society "truth" is being attacked. In the modern era, many philosophers and theologians deny the existence of objective reality or truth, saying: "Reality is in the mind of the beholder" or "We create our own truth." It should not surprise us that everyone has begun to doubt the fact of truth. Dr. Dave Miller says:

> *Perhaps the greatest deterrent to a proper interpretation of the Bible is the widespread and growing sense of uncertainty in the acquisition of absolute truth. American civilization has been inundated with pluralism, and has been brow-beaten into accepting the notion that one belief is as good as another and that it really does not matter what one believes.* [54]

In this study, we will follow the historical definition of truth, given above: *Truth is defined as that which conforms to reality.*

What then is our responsibility? It is to seek truth in God's Word, to endeavor to understand it, and to apply it in our lives. David said, "*O my God, I trust in thee… Lead me in thy truth, and teach me: for thou art the God of my salvation; on thee do I wait all the day*" (Ps 25:2,5). David had a tremendous respect for truth for he mentioned it often in the Psalms and he <u>actively</u> sought it from God. He says in Ps 119:94, "*I am thine, save me; for I have sought thy precepts.*"

Is it possible to misunderstand God's truth, what He has said in His Word? Very definitely. Even Bible scholars can misunderstand words, thoughts, and teaching from the Bible. Jesus' disciples spent three and a half years listening to Him, the greatest teacher that ever lived, and yet they misunderstood Him at least twice. Jesus met two of his disciples on the road to Emmaus and questioned them as to what they were talking about and why they were sad. They related to Him the recent events at Jerusalem saying,

---

[54] Apologetics Press: *Scripturally Speaking- The Bible is its Own Best Interpreter.* http://www.apologeticspress.org/articles/2293 (Accessed 12/2010)

The chief priests and our rulers delivered him to be condemned to death, and have crucified him. But we trusted that it had been he which should have redeemed Israel... (Luke 24:20,21).

A literal translation of verse 21 gives: *But we had hoped that he was the one to redeem Israel.*[55] Literally, this means their hope was now dead. It also means that they did not believe that the resurrection had taken place or could take place. Jesus was dead and all hope of the Kingdom was gone. It was evident that they had not understood the teaching of Jesus when He foretold His death and resurrection from the grave. He had clearly spoken on the issue several times and He had talked of it often in the hours leading up to the event. He had spoken the truth and they did not understand it even though they were face to face with Him and there was no problem of language or culture. They were hindered by their preconceived belief that His Kingdom was to come immediately.

A second occurrence of a clear misunderstanding of Jesus' teaching is found in Acts 1:6:

When they therefore were come together, they asked of him, saying, Lord, wilt thou at this time restore again the kingdom to Israel?

The disciples were looking to Him to chase out the Romans and to install His Kingdom immediately. Even though Jesus had never taught this, it was often in their thoughts. Though their thoughts had been turned completely upside down by His death, with the miraculous, supernatural fact of the resurrection, their expectation of a soon-to-be kingdom had resurfaced. However, in His teaching, Jesus had spoken to them many times of His plan for the *immediate* future and these plans did not include setting up His Kingdom on earth at that time. He was preparing them for a ministry that would take place after His return to Heaven. He had said *"My kingdom is not of this world"* and *"I go unto my father"* and *"I go to prepare a place for you."* His discussion with Peter in John 21 concerned that which Peter and John would do after His departure and before His return. And yet, they still asked Him in Acts 1:6, *"Wilt thou at this time restore again the kingdom to Israel?"* Though Daniel had clearly spoken of this over 400 years before, they did not understand that there would be a *delay* in the establishment of the Kingdom. We can understand why they did not put all this together in their minds: these instances are mentioned here only to show that it is possible to misunderstand even divine truth.

So what can we do? We must diligently seek to understand God's Word, respecting the miraculous nature of it and realizing that there are some special considerations for proper understanding of it. In this chapter we will briefly look at these considerations and apply them to our subject.

First, we need to define "interpretation." The popular meaning is "to find your own meaning for something." The Biblical meaning is "to unfold the meaning of what is said, to explain, to expound." A perfect example of this is Jesus' response to His disciples' misunderstanding on the road to Emmaus:

> *O fools, and slow of heart to believe all that the prophets have spoken:... And beginning at Moses and all the prophets, he "expounded" unto them in all the scriptures the things concerning himself.* Luke 24:25, 27.

Jesus' method of interpreting the truth about Himself was to give the entire context of God's revelation concerning Himself.

Secondly, in order to interpret a word or passage correctly, we must consider the following statement: if God has caused His message to be recorded in the Bible for mankind, then we would expect him to use human communication that is simple and understandable (i.e. propositional truth expressed in human language). Therefore when we interpret the Bible we must approach it as if it is God's plain word to us, spoken through His prophets in time-space history. It is to be taken literally and accepted completely unless the context indicates otherwise. Years ago my hermeneutics professor in Bible school summed up the practice of interpretation this way: *If the plain sense makes good sense, seek no other sense.*

Thirdly, we must consider the context of a word or passage. What is "context"?

1. *The circumstances that form the setting for an event, statement, or idea, and in terms of which it can be fully understood and assessed.*

2. *The parts of something written or spoken that immediately precede and follow a word or passage and clarify its meaning[56]*

Every word you read must be understood in the light of the words that come before the verse or verses, and the words that come after the particular verse or verses in question. Many passages will not be understood at all, or at least will be understood incorrectly, without the help afforded by the context.[57]

In biblical interpretation there are several contexts, and they must all be respected: grammatical, historical, theological, and Christological. We must understand not only the meaning of the word or phrase in the sentence or paragraph but also the meaning in the historical culture when it was written and the meaning in relation to other biblical teaching which concerns it. Careful attention should be given to its meaning,

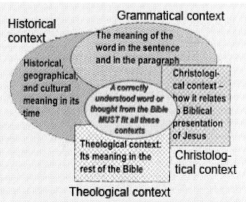

[56] http://www.google.com/search?q=definition+of+context&ie=utf-8&oe=utfwikipedia8&aq=t&rls=org.mozilla:en-US:official&client=firefox-a, (Accessed 8/10/2011).

[57] "The Eight Rules of Interpretation," Guy Duty. http://www.ancienthebrew.org/20_interpretation.html (Accessed 7/30/2011)

especially as it touches the teaching about Jesus. Just as a puzzle piece must fit all the sides which touch it, so the correct meaning will make sense when all the contexts that concern it agree.

Let's look at grammatical context. Words are grouped into sentences, paragraphs, and chapters for communication. They must be understood as they relate between themselves and this relation is called context. Consider an example from Scripture:

> *And in the vine were three branches: and it was as though it budded, and her blossoms shot forth; and the clusters thereof brought forth ripe grapes: And Pharaoh's cup was in my hand: and I took the grapes, and pressed them into Pharaoh's cup, and I gave the cup into Pharaoh's hand (Genesis 40:10,11).*

That which was squeezed into Pharaoh's cup was quite certainly grape juice, from the context (surrounding phrases). It would be foolish to understand anything else. The butler took "grapes" and "squeezed" them. The result can only be grape juice, not fermented wine. Yet, even here there is a problem. Josephus, an educated 1st century Jewish historian, told the story of Pharaoh's cup and called this product "*oinos*" or wine. The solution is that the Greek word *oinos* was a generic word in Josephus' time which, besides the sense of an alcoholic beverage, included the primary sense of fresh grape juice.

Another example of respecting the context of written words is the biblical word, winepress. This word was used historically to describe an enclosure in which grapes were put to be trampled so that the juice could run out and be captured. The Bible speaks of "*the fulness of the winepress*" (Num 18:27) and "*the increase of the winepress*" (Num 18:30). This fullness or increase can only mean fresh grape juice as it was the first product of the raw material, grapes. Therefore, a "wine press" was actually a "grape press." We see that the historical context is vital here.

I repeat again for emphasis: Just as a puzzle piece must fit ALL the sides which touch it, so the correct meaning will make sense when ALL the contexts that concern it agree. *"When all the facts of an interpretation are in agreement they sound together in harmony, like notes in a chord."*[58]

Besides this basic rule of respecting the context, thoughtful Bible scholars have developed certain rules down through the centuries that help interpret Scripture. This is because it must be interpreted differently than other ancient writings as it is a supernatural book. These rules of biblical Interpretation will be listed here and briefly applied in the study of grape juice in the Bible.

1. God's WORD is spiritually discerned, you must be born again to understand it.

This is simple, logical, and biblical. If a person has not accepted God's gift of salvation which is provided as a result of Christ's sacrificial death on the cross, he cannot understand God's revelation.

> *But the natural man receiveth not the things of the Spirit of God: for they are foolishness unto him: neither can he know them, because they are <u>spiritually</u> discerned,* 1 Cor. 2:14.

It was Calvin who noted -- and the apostle Paul who stated in 1 Corinthians 2:14-15 -- that the Word of God is *spiritual,* and, therefore, can only be perceived and discerned by the spiritual man:

> *The Bible can very clearly be understood when: [1] We are born again-- personal faith in the Son of God; [2] we are empowered and enabled by the Spirit of God-- 'not grieving, not quenching, and walking by means of the Spirit'-- Eph. 4:30, 1 Thes. 5:19, and Gal. 5:16; and [3] we approach with an attitude of humility, in simple child-like faith.* [59]

---

[58] *The Eight Rules of Interpretation,* Guy Duty. *Ibid.*
[59] http://www.theologue.org/hermbiblicl-ramm.htm (Accessed 11/20/2010).

There is a tremendous amount of discussion on the internet concerning the subject of grape juice in the Bible. Many of those who "post" on the internet make no pretense of being born again nor do they accept God's word as being inspired truth. Some of these "experts" are quoted by Christian writers. We should not consult such experts much less accept their conclusions.

2. God's WORD is God-given – inspired, inerrant, and preserved for us.

The Bible is not a book that we can approach as other ancient writings where we can make the author say what seems sensible to us.

> *All scripture is given by inspiration of God... For the prophecy came not in old time by the will of man: but holy men of God spake as they were moved by the Holy Ghost. For whatsoever things were written aforetime were written for our learning, that we through patience and <u>comfort</u> of the scriptures might have hope.* 2Timothy 3:16, 2 Peter 1:21, Romans 15:4.

These excerpts from the verses mean that the Bible was written in ancient times by men who were so controlled by God that what they wrote was exactly what God wanted them to write. This means also that God did not make any mistakes in the Bible in the original autographs, even in the words that He used. Jesus authenticated all the Hebrew letters that composed the Old Testament: *"I say unto you, Till heaven and earth pass, one jot or one tittle shall in no wise pass from the law"* (Matthew 5:18). We can never say that God used the wrong word in the Bible. We must only try to understand what He meant by the words He used. Andrew Kulikovsky says:

> *The doctrine of Biblical Inspiration is fundamental to evangelical Christianity. Without this essential notion, the uniqueness and authority of the Bible is destroyed. The Bible just becomes one of*

many ancient books and the truths of historic Christianity are reduced to a collection of religious myths. [60]

3. God's WORD is progressive – it builds from the account of the creation to the prophecies of Revelation.

Heb 1:1,2 says: *"God, who at sundry times and in divers manners spake in time past unto the fathers by the prophets, Hath in these last days spoken unto us by his Son…"* The sense of this verse is that God spoke in the past and spoke more fully by His Son after the Incarnation. We better understand Jesus' words because of God's revelation prior to His coming. Without going into details about the different historical situations in which God spoke to man, we will simply affirm that Abraham understood more of what God said to him than Noah would have, and that Paul understood a great deal more than Moses, because much more of God's revelation was available to him. Of course we can understand infinitely more than the Jews who listened to Jesus because we have the entire New Testament to add to the Old. Accepting this principle of Biblical Interpretation is vital to understanding Scripture.

There is a definite progression in Scripture, and unless this principle of progress is recognized there can be no clear exegesis of Scripture. Progressive revelation means that as the timeline of history unravels, the plan and purpose of God becomes fuller and clearer; the meat is slowly being put on the bones, if you will. . [61]

[60] http://hermeneutics.kulikovskyonline.net/hermeneutics/inspirat.htm (Accessed 11/29/2010).
[61] http://www.theologue.org/hermbiblicl-ramm.htm from Bernard Ramm's writings on Biblical Interpretation. (Accessed 11/29/2010).

4. God's WORD is one complete REVELATION – God is the author of ALL of it and this is what He has to say to us.

We must never forget that in the Bible, it is God who is speaking. He simply cannot say something in one part of Scripture that contradicts what He has said in another part of scripture. He must be consistent. The Bible covers centuries of time. For instance, there are over five hundred years between Moses' writings and the book of Isaiah. God, the author of all Scripture, knew what He had said before Isaiah wrote by inspiration, and He meant His truth to continue until our time and beyond. *"For the LORD is good; his mercy is everlasting; and his truth endureth to all generations"* Psalms 100:5. We affirm that the words and truths that He uses in one part of Scripture must agree with everything He has said in all of Scripture, for He must always be consistent.

This fourth rule of Bible Interpretation is taught clearly in the Bible by two words: *all* and Scripture. It is **all Scripture** that is given by inspiration of God, which is profitable to correct us and teach us God's way. Jesus corrected the thinking of the two disciples on the road to Emmaus by going back through **all Scripture** and He used those two words in His teaching: *"beginning at Moses and all the prophets, he expounded unto them in **all** the **scriptures** the things concerning himself"* (Luke 24:27). *Scripture* is the translation of the Greek word for *writing.* Geisler says:

> *The New Testament uses the term Scripture in a technical sense. It occurs some fifty times, and in most cases it refers unmistakably to the Old Testament as a whole. To first-century Christians, the*

word Scripture meant primarily the canon of the Old Testament, which is called "sacred" (2 Tim. 3:15) or "holy" (Rom. 1:2). [62]

Jesus clearly emphasized the importance of *all Scripture*. He spoke often about an act or a word saying that it happened in order that Scripture *might be fulfilled*. This was even more important as His death approached for He used the entire phrase *Scripture might be fulfilled* three times in John 17 and 19. For Jesus, not just phrases or words of Scripture were God given and vital, but even the letters. In Mat 5:18 He said, *"For verily I say unto you, Till heaven and earth pass, one jot or one tittle shall in no wise pass from the law, till all be fulfilled."*

Another Scriptural word that describes God's perfect consistency throughout His entire revelation is "faithful": *Know therefore that the LORD thy God, he is God, the faithful God, which keepeth covenant, Deut. 7:9, "To affirm that God is consistent means He never becomes greater, better, or worse; He never learns, grows, develops, improves, evolves, or gets younger or older"* [63] We can further say:

> *God's nature, plans and actions do not change even though he is active and his relationships do not remain static. His moral consistency guarantees his commitment to unchanging principles.* [64]

In our interpretation of the biblical word *wine* we must find an understanding that must work in **every** single case. This is clearly not the case in the current popular understanding that it always means an alcoholic beverage.

[62] Geisler, N. L., & Nix, W. E. (1996). *A General Introduction to the Bible* (Rev. and expanded.) (76–77). Chicago: Moody Press.

[63] Dockery, D. S., Butler, T. C., Church, C. L., Scott, L. L., Ellis Smith, M. A., White, J. E., & Holman Bible Publishers (Nashville, T. (1992). *Holman Bible Handbook* (812). Nashville, TN: Holman Bible Publishers.

[64] *Zondervan Dictionary of Bible Themes*

5. God's WORD is clear - meant to be understood

God says in Isaiah 45:19, *"I have not spoken in secret, in a dark place of the earth: I said not unto the seed of Jacob, Seek ye me in vain: I the LORD speak righteousness* [what is just, normal, or true], *I declare things that are right."* This is a very important principle. Bernard Ramm said: *"The Bible was given to us in the form of human language and therefore appeals to human reason - it invites investigation."*[65] Martin Luther believed that, in a physical sense, one could clearly understand the plain teaching of Scripture in applying regular rules of grammar and hermeneutics to the text of Scripture. He added that there was always a spiritual sense in which the believer is aided by the illumination of the Holy Spirit.

Not only did God give His Revelation to be understood, but He also interprets it for us! The following quote is from Ramm's book on Biblical Interpretation:

> *Around the time of the Reformation the Roman Catholic Church insisted that it was 'gifted with the grace of interpretation,' and therefore, it knew instinctively the interpretation of Scripture. The Reformers rejected this erroneous claim and set in its place the rule that Scripture is its own interpreter-- Scriptura sacra sui ipsius interpres... What it means, very simply, is that the Bible as a whole interprets the various parts, and hence no single aspect of the Word can be so interpreted as to destroy the teaching of the whole.*[66]

This very basic rule of Biblical Interpretation simply reinforces the application of the preceding hermeneutical rules that we have applied to the understanding of grape juice in the Bible. Not only does God

---

[65] Ramm is cited in an excellent article, *The Eight Rules of Interpretation*, Guy Duty. http://www.ancient-hebrew.org/20_interpretation.html (Accessed 7/30/2011)
[66] http://www.theologue.org/hermbiblicl-ramm.htm, (Accessed 12/2010).

never contradict Himself, but consulting two separate passages on a given subject helps us to come to a full understanding of both.

In Nehemiah 10:37, the order is given to: *"bring the firstfruits of our dough, and our offerings, and the fruit of all manner of trees, of wine and of oil, unto the priests, to the chambers of the house of our God..."*

This verse is especially interesting. It tells the Jews to bring "wine" to the priests, into the house of God. But there is a seeming contradiction here with another Scripture for, according to Leviticus 10:9, God gave a command to the priests which carried with it a severe punishment if broken:

> *Do not drink wine nor strong drink, thou, nor thy sons with thee, when ye go into the tabernacle of the congregation, lest ye die: it shall be a statute forever throughout your generations.*

Ezekiel repeats this prohibition in 44:21: *"Neither shall any priest drink wine, when they enter into the inner court."* And yet, Neh. 10:37 records the instruction: *"... we should bring the firstfruits of our dough, and our offerings, and the fruit of all manner of trees, of wine and of oil, unto the priests, to the chambers of the house of our God..."* God would seem to say in the two passages: *"Priests must not drink wine in the temple"* and *"you must bring wine into the temple for the priests."* Since God is always consistent and cannot contradict Himself, we must understand that He is talking about two different substances: the "wine" in Leviticus and Ezekiel must be fermented and the "wine" in Nehemiah must be grape juice! In the case of Nehemiah's order to bring the wine into the Temple, we are helped to understand by the fact that the Hebrew word for wine is "tirosh" which means literally "unfermented grape juice."

There are, of course, a great many other examples of God's Word interpreting itself and making things clear for us. There is a particular question which is often raised today: How can God mislead us concerning the truths about fermented wine in the Bible if the word in

68

our English Bible does not give a clear sense? The answer is to study God's Word – all of God's Word. Paul says *"Study to shew thyself approved unto God, a workman that needeth not to be ashamed, rightly dividing the word of truth"* (2 Tim 2:15). When we consider the added meaning that comes from the Greek, we have: *"Study diligently to shew thyself approved unto God, a workman that needeth not to be ashamed, rightly dividing* **(to cut straight, to proceed on straight paths, hold a straight course, to handle aright, to teach the truth directly and correctly)** *the word of truth."*

6. God's WORD has one principal subject – Jesus Christ.

In the Old Testament, Jesus is the promised Messiah from Genesis to Malachi. In the Gospels, Jesus is "Emmanuel" or God with us and "the Lamb of God, which taketh away the sin of the world." In the rest of the New Testament, Jesus and His coming are preached and taught. Paul *"preached unto them Jesus, and the resurrection"* (Ac 17:18). It is absolutely vital that this rule of Bible Interpretation be respected. The *Chicago Statement on Biblical Hermeneutics* puts it this way:

> *The Person and work of Jesus Christ are the central focus of the entire Bible... This Affirmation follows the teaching of Christ that He is the central theme of Scripture (Matt. 5:17; Luke 24:27, 44; John 5:39; Heb. 10:7). This is to say that focus on the person and work of Christ runs throughout the Bible from Genesis to Revelation.* [67]

The life and ministry of Jesus are abundantly narrated in the New Testament, but they are also clearly foretold in the Old Testament, through prophecy as well as pictures and symbols that God used. God

---

[67] Summit I of the International Council on Biblical Inerrancy took place in Chicago on October 26-28, 1978 for the purpose of affirming afresh the doctrine of the inerrancy of Scripture... *Explaining Hermeneutics: A Commentary on the Chicago Statement on Biblical Hermeneutics.* Oakland, California: International Council on Biblical Inerrancy, 1983.

revealed to Moses exactly what He wanted in the Tabernacle and the sacrifices. The overall message of these symbols is that Jesus is holy and that the Holy One was to be a perfect sacrifice for the sins of His people.

How does this tenet of Biblical Interpretation help us in our study of grape juice? Actually it is of crucial importance. Let us look at just two events in the life of Christ.

Jesus and the Lord's Supper. The first event that needs to be considered, the Passover Supper, took place just before His death and resurrection. If there is no grape juice in the Bible, then Jesus drank an alcoholic beverage there with His disciples, and He did so against all the typology in the Old Testament. When He instituted the Lord's Supper for His disciples and for the Church, He partook of what is called the fruit of the vine. Since there was grape juice in Bible times, it is very clear that this is that to which He was referring, because the fruit of the vine, or grape juice, contained no leaven. Jesus was celebrating the Passover with his disciples and God had very specific commandments for celebrating the Passover. The *Pulpit Commentary* says*: "No leavened bread was to be eaten during that space, and leaven was even to be put away altogether out of all houses."* [68] Actually, we must go further and affirm that all sacrifices in the Old Testament prefigured Christ's sacrifice and were "without leaven," which was a type of sin. Leavening (Hebrew, *Chametz*) refers to a grain product that is already fermented (i.e. yeast breads, certain types of cake and most alcoholic beverages). The Torah commandments regarding chametz are:

To remove all chametz from one's home, including things made with chametz, before the first day of Passover. (Exodus 12:15).

To refrain from eating chametz or mixtures containing chametz during Passover. (Exodus 13:3, Exodus 12:20, Deuteronomy 16:3).

---

[68] *The Pulpit Commentary: Exodus (Vol. 1)* , Ex. 11.10.

Not to possess chametz in one's domain (i.e. home, office, car, etc.) during Passover (Exodus 12:19, Deuteronomy 16:4).

The orthodox Jews to this day make a ceremony of searching out leaven in their homes. John Moss says:

Since leaven is a critical component of fermentation, drinking alcoholic wine would violate the Jewish tradition and God's instructions for the Jews. Many Jews, in order to obey God's command, would press out fresh grapes out into cups or pitchers themselves just prior to consumption to make certain that the juice was not fermented.[69]

There can be no doubt as to the presence of yeast in intoxicating wine. Here are two references from articles on making wine:

The fermentation process, step four, is where the juice becomes wine. Special yeast, added to the juice, converts the natural sugars into alcohol.

To start primary fermentation, yeast is added to the must for red wine or juice for white wine. During this fermentation, which often takes between one and two weeks, the yeast converts most of the sugars in the grape juice into ethanol (alcohol) and carbon dioxide. The carbon dioxide is lost to the atmosphere.[70]

Not only does the interpretation of "the fruit of the vine" as being fermented at the Last Supper cause a problem with the typology of the Passover, but it causes a great problem in looking forward to the Millennial Kingdom. Jesus said, "*I will not drink henceforth of this fruit of the vine, until that day when I drink it new with you in my Father's Kingdom*" (Mat. 26:26). Will alcohol then be a problem in the Kingdom?

---

[69] http://www.associatedcontent.com/article/784631/was_jesus_a_brewer.html?singlepage=true-&cat=22 (used by permission of author).
[70] http://www.winemaking.com/; http://en.wikipedia.org/wiki/Winemaking (Accessed 12/06/2010).

Jesus' creation of "wine." The second event that needs to be considered is found in the narrative of Jesus' first miracle at Cana of Galilee. Here, Jesus made water into "wine," which a great many modern-day preachers, Bible teachers, and laymen use to legitimize moderate drinking for Christians today.

There is no question of the importance of the interpretation of this passage. Peter Lumpkins says:

> *Indisputably the nail most often driven to morally fasten the recreational consumption of intoxicating beverages into a solid ethical structure originates in the New Testament. The Founder of Christianity Himself, the Second Person of the Blessed Trinity, God in human flesh--Jesus Christ--becomes the moderationist model. His practice, they say, unmistakably included consuming intoxicating beverages himself, and that, in the text before us, actually creating intoxicating beverages for others to consume.*[71]

We must ask the question here, was not the "wine" that Jesus created really grape juice?

The fact that all Scripture has as a primary subject, the person of Jesus Christ (perfect God, sinless man) will help us to decide the meaning of "wine" in this context. The whole truth about Jesus' first miracle, in John 2, will clarify the issue.

First, Jesus knew the Old Testament Scriptures. He astounded the learned Jews in the temple at the age of 12. He certainly knew what God said about the effects of alcohol:

> *Wine is a mocker, strong drink is raging; and whosoever is deceived is not wise... (Proverbs 20:1).*

> *Who hath woe? who hath sorrow? who hath contentions? who hath babbling? who hath wounds without cause? who hath redness of eyes? They that tarry long at the wine;...(Proverbs 23:29).*

---

[71] Peter Lumpkins, *op. cit.*, p. 141

Can we imagine that Jesus wanted to produce this effect at the marriage feast? He also would have known specifically the instruction of Habakkuk 2:15:

> *Woe unto him that giveth his neighbour drink, that puttest thy bottle to him, and makes him drunken also, that thou mayest look on their nakedness!*

Obviously the prophet here is talking about the alcoholic beverage made from grape juice. If "wine" in the Bible always means this alcoholic beverage, then Jesus made a drink which certainly contributed to drunkenness. According to God's condemnation He was at fault for such an act.

There is an equivalent warning about causing people to stumble in Romans 14:21: *"It is good neither to eat flesh, nor to drink wine, nor any thing whereby thy brother stumbleth, or is offended, or is made weak."*

In the story of this miracle, the master of the feast says, *"Every man at the beginning doth set forth good wine; and when men have well drunk, then that which is worse" (John 2:10).* If a person drinks even diluted wine until he has "well drunk," more alcohol will add to the content in his blood and he will be on his way to being drunken.

We have only two possibilities in understanding "wine" in this passage:

1. If they were already drinking unfermented grape juice and He created fresh grape juice, He would have shown His Divine power in creating instantly a natural drink and they could have STILL tasted grape juice that was BETTER than what they had had!

2. But if they were already drinking alcoholic wine and they were "well-drunk" (John says so), and Jesus made more for them, then He created a man-made corruption of a natural drink that

made them DRUNKER and incapable of knowing that the created drink was better than what they had already had.

The knowledge of His Holy person and calling make it certain that Jesus would never have created a substance that is systematically condemned in the Old Testament. We must never forget the reason for **all** of Jesus' miracles – to demonstrate His divine power and glory. In fact the inspired comment on this miracle is found at the end of the story, John 2:11: *This beginning of miracles did Jesus in Cana of Galilee, and manifested forth his glory; and his disciples believed on him.*

In this chapter we began with God's statement *"For the word of the LORD is right; and all his works are done in truth"* (Ps 33:4). God's truth has been given us and we have the responsibility to interpret or understand it correctly. This means to compare Scripture with Scripture, for God often interprets it for us. It also means to respect all of its contexts, grammatical, historical, theological, and Christological. When we do this, we can answer with assurance the question: "is there grape juice in the Bible?" The answer is an unequivocal "yes" and following chapters will only confirm it.

At the opening of this chapter I spoke of a conversation that I had with a hermeneutics professor who would always answer an emphatic "no" to the possibility that grape juice existed in the Bible. At the end of our time together, after he had rejected all the reasons for affirming "yes," he said: "If you can send me just one proof from an ancient source that I can accept, I will change my mind." After arriving home I did a study on one Hebrew word, *tirosh,* from the Old Testament and that word is always translated "wine" in the English Bible.[72] The Bible is the oldest and most dependable ancient source available and the Hebrew word "tirosh," when properly translated can only mean "fresh grape juice." I also pointed out that reliable French and Italian Bibles translated tirosh by a word meaning "must" or freshly squeezed grape juice. I sent this example to him. Unfortunately he would not accept this proof.

---

[72] Part of the results of which are found on page 17 & 18 of this book.

IX. Wrongly Interpreting "Wine" -- A Popular Error: "The Diluted Wine Theory"

There is a very popular and widespread error in our time, the diluted wine theory. Those who hold to this theory interpret "wine" in the Bible to be a diluted alcoholic beverage in every passage where God seems to bless "wine" but to be undiluted when God condemns the use thereof. They explain at great length that in Bible times the wine was not nearly as intoxicating as that of today even when it was full strength. Furthermore, according to them, drinking it at that time without diluting it was a social error. Probably the most widely read author of this theory is Norman Geisler in *A Christian Perspective on Wine Drinking* (in Bibliotheca Sacra, Vol. 139, 1982). Here is a summary of his position:

- *The Bible does not teach that New Testament communion wine was unfermented. All wine was fermented wine. Some Corinthians were drunk at the Lord's Table (cf. 1 Cor. 11:21), which would be very difficult to accomplish if the wine was unfermented.*
- *The Bible does not teach that "new wine" was unfermented. Hosea 4:11 says that both "old wine" and "new wine" take away understanding. And Acts 2:13 tells of how the Spirit-filled believers were accused of drunkenness, being filled with new wine.*
- *It is false to say that Jesus made unfermented wine (compare John 2:9-10 with Mark 2:22 and Eph. 5:18).*
- *It is incorrect to say that the New Testament teaches that first-century Christians were not to use wine at any time.*
- *It is a myth to say that total abstinence was a New Testament condition for church membership.*[73]

---

[73] *Is Drinking Alcohol Allowed for a Christian?* http://blog.davidrhoades.org /2008_06_01_archive.html. (Accessed 7/31/2011).

His whole argument is based on the presupposition that "wine" is always alcoholic, and he ignores both historical, etymological[74], and biblical evidence against his position. We will examine several arguments against this interpretation.

1. Historical evidence against "The Diluted Wine Theory"

Much of the "proof" for this theory is an interpretation of historical references that ignores the fact that grape juice syrup was also served by adding water to it. This theory assumes that every time ancient writers talk of adding water they are talking about alcohol. Based on his work, New Testament scholar Robert Stein really exaggerates the theory by saying that wine in the New Testament was essentially purified water: He gives as proof the following statements:

* Wine in Homer's day was twenty parts water to one part wine.
* Pliny referred to wine as eight parts water to one part wine.
* Aristophanes: three parts water to two parts wine.
* Euenos: three parts water to one part wine.
* Hesiod: three parts water to one part wine.
* Alexis: four parts water to one part wine.
* Diocles and Anacreon: two parts water to one part wine.
* Ion: three parts water to one part wine.
* Strong wine was typically considered to be one part water to one part wine.[75]

A great many modern authors take up this refrain with varying statistics and emphasis.

It is very true that the ancient peoples around the Mediterranean Sea diluted the product of the vine, both alcoholic wine and grape juice. An example of a modern method of creating grape juice syrup is given on page 35. This process produces concentrated syrup to which water is

---

[74] Etymology is the study of the *history* of *words*, their origins, and how their form and *meaning* have changed over time.
[75] *Is Drinking Alcohol Allowed for a Christian?*, op. cit.

76

normally added and goes back as far in history as vineyards and grape juice. The story of Abigail previously presented also shows the practice of adding water to grape syrup. Many of the historical references given in Stein's list to support the "diluted wine theory" could very well have referred to concentrated grape syrup with water.

2. Cultural evidence against "The Diluted Wine Theory"

The assumption that "diluted wine" is always a weak alcoholic drink is untenable in the light of the knowledge of the Old Testament culture. Throughout the biblical presentation of Israel and the Promised Land, there is the description of a special people living in a special land, with conditions that were to be totally different from those of the people around them. God prepared and called out this special people to have a special relationship with Him. In Lev. 20:26, God says: *"And ye shall be holy unto me: for I the LORD am holy, and have severed you from other people, that ye should be mine."* He played a large part in determining certain aspects of their culture. They were to love Him and follow His words in obedience while He promised certain blessings to them if they followed Him.

First, God promised a new land to His people when He took them out of slavery in Egypt. He provided this land, according to His promise.

Secondly, God promised protection of His people, as evidenced by David's statement in Psalms 121:7,8:

> *The LORD shall preserve thee from all evil: he shall preserve thy soul. The LORD shall preserve thy going out and thy coming in from this time forth, and even for evermore.*

Finally, God promised to provide for the needs of His people. Running through the Old Testament, God talked of His provision in terms of natural and healthy products. Two examples of this are the promises to Jacob and to Judah. To Jacob He said, *"Therefore God give thee of the dew of heaven, and the fatness of the earth, and plenty of corn and wine"* (Gen 27:28). He told Judah (in Jacob's death-bed blessing to his children) that his inheritance would have both vines and grape juice ("the blood of the grape") in Gen 49:11.

In all, in the Old Testament, God mentioned bread 255 times, oil 176, fruit or fruit trees 126, corn 86, flour 56, wheat 40, and grapes 30 times. The English word "wine" is found 212 times in the Old Testament and is a translation of seven different Hebrew words. Thirty-one times we find "corn and wine" in a list of several other products mentioned. Twenty-eight times the Hebrew word "tirosh" is used in those lists, which means fresh grape juice (page 18).

The God of the Jews promised His people a land which would provide grapes and grape juice. He then provided them with these products and protected them in their land while they enjoyed these products.

3. Scientific and biblical evidence against "The Diluted Wine Theory"

One very popular tenet of the "The Diluted Wine Theory" is that diluted alcoholic wine was needed to purify water during Bible times. This idea is expressed in many articles on the worldwide web, and it is often used by Christian writers who have not considered its problems. Garrett Peck, author of *The Prohibition Hangover* (and a freelance writer for the alcoholic beverage industry) says:

> *The ancients didn't understand microbes and gastrointestinal disease, but they knew that drinking water led to sickness and sometimes death. The water supply was often contaminated, particularly around settlements that had no sanitation, or even in short supply during droughts. So they drank wine but diluted it with water, both to quench the thirst and to dilute the effects of such strong drink. This kept them healthy. In fact, the phrase "strong drink" in the Bible may refer to undiluted wine.* [76]

---

[76] http://prohibitionhangover.com/israelwine.html (Accessed 12/07/2010).

Even though he is not a believer in God's inspired Word, that which he espouses so learnedly is repeated by a great many writers who promote the idea of Christians drinking moderately.

The point that people in Bible times supposedly did not have safe drinking water and therefore required alcohol to make it safe is an important point for those who teach that grape juice is never spoken of in the Bible.

To make drinking water safe by adding fermented grape juice would be a very laborious process for each family. There is no historical evidence that families needed to purify drinking water in such a fashion. Boiling water for drinking would have been much easier than preparing enough wine to purify it. As missionaries in Africa, we boiled our water.

It would be well to consider some of the implications of the theory that diluted wine made safe drinking water for God's people.

One such implication concerns the Israelites during their wilderness wanderings. It is unlikely that there could be found enough grapes to process to make enough wine to purify water for the whole congregation for a period of 40 years.

Another implication concerns Israel in the Promised Land at the time of David's numbering of the people. When David ordered Joab to number Israel (2 Samuel 24:10) he found 1,250,000 men of war. We can conservatively estimate the population of Israel with women and children during that time to be at least 4 million. The human body needs approximately 32 oz. of water per day. Even at a 50% mixture of 4% alcohol and water it is impossible that unsafe water would become safe.[77] If we assume that it would then be safe anyway, this would necessitate 10 to 15 oz. of wine per day for 4 million people: at just 10 oz. per day, this makes 20 million U.S. quarts of wine made and

---

[77] I spoke with an expert at safewater.org who laughed when I asked her what percentage of alcohol would have to be added to make unsafe water safe. She said 100%!

consumed per day! This one calculation makes this theory absolutely untenable.

That there *was* safe drinking water *can* be shown from Scripture. The Bible says, for instance, in Gen 16:7: *"And the angel of the LORD found her by a fountain of water in the wilderness."* This was obviously water to drink. Later Abraham gave Hagar a bottle of water and sent her away with her child (Gen. 21:14). Then Rebekah gave Abraham's servant water to drink out of a well (Gen 24:19). The Bible is full of such references. In fact, Proverbs 5:15 speaks clearly about safe water: *"Drink waters out of thine own cistern, and running waters out of thine own well."*

R.A. Baker says:

> *I have read a good many documents of first and second century writers. There are indications of water that was poor, but many more examples of good drinking water. Well water was common, the collection of rain water for drinking was common – the Bible has numerous examples of people drinking water. In the midst of [his] lengthy discourse on wine Pliny admits, ... "more labour is spent [on wine] – as if nature had not given us the most healthy of beverages to drink, water, which all other animals make use of..."*[78]

Moreover, we would ask some very disturbing questions of those who affirm that people in Bible times mixed fermented wine with unsafe water to make it safe. For instance, *"Would it have been healthy for pregnant mothers to drink that much alcohol?"* *"How about children?"* *"Why were the Nazirites and the Rechabites denied the protection of mixing wine with their water?"*

Whether intoxicating wine was diluted in Bible times has no bearing on the question of whether or not grape juice existed at that time and was available. We know that concentrated grape juice was mixed with water from the story of Abigail and the feast she brought David and his

[78] R.A. Baker, *Wine in the Ancient World*, www.churchhistory101.com/docs/ Wine-Ancient-World.pdf, (Accessed 10/13/09)

men (see page 20). We also know that people got drunk on biblical "wine," proving that their wine had sufficient alcohol for drunkenness.

4. *Hermeneutical evidence against "The Diluted Wine Theory"*

In Chapter II it was shown that the word "wine" in the Bible is a generic word which is used to refer to several different Hebrew words meaning grape juice or alcoholic wine. We have presented arguments showing that the Diluted Wine Theory is a wrong interpretation of biblical "wine." Now we want to consider the phrase, "wine and strong drink" as used in Scripture.

A proper interpretation of this phrase will reveal the "diluted wine theory" as fallacy. The popular teaching is that "wine" in the Bible is usually diluted and that "strong drink" then would indicate undiluted wine. In the English Bible, the Hebrew word for this drink, is *shaycawr*, and has been translated by the two words "strong drink."

> As to the words "strong drink" in our common version, it may here be well to remark, that there are not two words in the original, but only the one word, "Shecar" or "Shaycaw." One learned author says, that the primitive idea of meaning of the word is—"sweetness," and this "sweet drink," as he renders it, was produced from the palm tree.[79]

This term is wrongly understood by some modern writers to refer to strong alcoholic content. In fact, some translate it "intoxicating drink." This incorrect translation is a result of failure to apply Bible etymology. Just as the word "wine" in the Bible is generic, so also is "strong drink." It can refer to a grain drink or a palm drink and either could be fermented or not.

---

[79] George Marshall, *op. cit.*, p. 15.

Shaycawr, or "strong drink" in the Authorized Version, is mentioned 20 times in the Old Testament. Except for one, every verse that contains it speaks also of "wine," usually as a synonym. Sometimes its use is condemned and sometimes it is condoned. This would prove that in each case they are either both alcoholic or both non-alcoholic. The first case is clearly shown through many references. For instance, Isaiah spoke of both wine and strong drink in Is. 28:7: *"But they also have erred through wine, and through strong drink are out of the way; the priest and the prophet have erred through strong drink, they are swallowed up of wine, they are out of the way through strong drink; they err in vision, they stumble in judgment."* Both of these terms are synonyms in the sense that their effects are harmful.

There are also many references which refer to both of these drinks as being beneficial and non-alcoholic. God told His people to pour this drink (Shaycawr) out before Him as a drink offering in Numbers 28:7, and we know there was to be no leaven in drink offerings. In Deuteronomy 14:26, it is included in the list of acceptable things they could bring before Him to eat or drink as an act of worship:

> *And thou shalt bestow that money for whatsoever thy soul lusteth after, for oxen, or for sheep, or for wine, or for strong drink, or for whatsoever thy soul desireth: and thou shalt eat there before the LORD thy God, and thou shalt rejoice, thou, and thine household.*

This makes no sense if Shaycawr referred to a "strong" alcoholic beverage as most Christian writers propose. Remember, the writers who promote the "one-wine" theory believe that God only blessed wine diluted with water and that Shaycawr, or "strong drink," represented undiluted wine. This is not true according to the meaning of Shaycawr, and it is not true according to Bible usage. God commanded His people to drink both Shaycawr and "wine" before His altar! We must understand that "strong drink" in the Old Testament referred to a sweet drink which was generally not fermented but could be. It was not a product of the vine. Many pastors who have accepted the current "diluted wine" teaching are simply unaware that *Shaycawr* is mentioned *with* wine in Scripture as an acceptable offering to God.

The mixture of gleanings from ancient writings and the modern rationale which is found in the Diluted Wine Theory solves no problem in the understanding of "wine" in the Bible. The Bible is the inerrant, inspired Revelation of the Holy God who clearly condemns intoxicating wine. The analysis of the Jewish culture and the historical situation of God's people finds no place for the widespread use of alcoholic beverages, no matter how diluted. Alcohol does not fit with the other basic, natural, healthy products that God provided for His people. Diluting a glass of intoxicating wine still leaves a percentage of alcohol in the drink and alcohol is a poison for the human system.

In our discussion of the sacrifices, we talked about the necessity of making sure there was no leaven present in those sacrifices. When we talk about the presence or absence of *leaven* or yeast in the drink offerings it matters little whether or not the alcohol was diluted. Leaven was always present in diluted alcohol, therefore the sacrifice would not be acceptable and the diluted wine theory is once again proved erroneous.

X. A Growing Problem with Alcohol

Even those who espouse the use of alcohol in moderation must agree that alcohol is an enormous problem in our modern culture. The list of comments about its dangers given previously on page 4 shows the seriousness of this social ill in our time. Even more frightening than the actual dangers that the consumption of alcohol creates in society is the fact that society in America has rapidly and fundamentally changed its attitude towards this consumption. Startling differences can be seen between the early 1900's, 1950-1980, and the early 2000's. Even greater changes can be foreseen as the problem worsens.

Societal and Christian attitudes toward alcoholic consumption in the early 1900's

During the 100 years before 1900, a fierce battle was waged between those engaged in either the sale or consumption of alcoholic beverages (including some church leaders) and the citizens, churches, and Christian organizations who were against it. The issue was hotly debated, especially among those in religious circles. We have seen in a preceding chapter that the "wets" (proponents of alcoholic consumption) were quite categorical in their attacks on the "dries" (proponents of temperance).

The "dries" were militantly against the consumption of alcohol. They spoke vehemently against the "modern" biblical interpretation of their time which trumpeted that "wine" in the Bible was always alcoholic. They wrote and spoke at length on the subject. Three quotations from Eliphalet Nott in 1847 will serve to illustrate their teachings:

That the fruit of the vine, in the form of grape juice as expressed from the cluster, has been from remote antiquity and still is used

84

as a beverage, is abundantly in proof. [80]

Concerning God's blessing and condemning the same substance, Nott says:

Can the same thing in the same state be good and bad, a symbol of wrath, a symbol of mercy, a thing to be sought after, a thing to be avoided? Certainly not! [81]

Then he asks a question and gives the answer,

And is the Bible then inconsistent with itself? No it is not, and this seeming inconsistency will vanish, and the Bible will be not only, but will appear to be in harmony with itself, in harmony with history, with science, and with the providence of God... [82]

A popular evangelist, writing on the subject of wine in 1980, characterized the earlier era by saying:

Many books were written during that period, some of which were by reputable Hebrew and Greek scholars who set forth solid evidence showing that the major words that were translated "wine" in Scripture (Hebrew yayin, Greek oinos) could mean either fermented or unfermented grape juice. [83]

Peter Lumpkins quoted John J. Owens about the drinking practices of Jesus, saying: *"as wine was a common beverage in that land of vineyards, in its unfermented state, our Lord most likely drank it. But that he did so in its intoxicating forms or that he indulged to excess in*

---

[80] Nott, Eliphalet, *Lectures on Biblical Temperance*, Turner & Co, London, 1963; p.68. (Available from Google Books).

[81] *Ibid*, p. 48

[82] *Ibid*, p. 53

[83] Van Impe, J., *Alcohol The Beloved Enemy*, Thomas Nelson Publishers, Nashville, 1980; p. 7.

its use in any form, was a false and malicious libel upon his character. "[84]

Most evangelical churches responded to the teaching of that era. In 1896 the Southern Baptists passed this resolution:

> *Furthermore, we announce it as the sense of this body that no person should be retained in the fellowship of a Baptist church who engages in the manufacture or sale of alcoholic liquors, or who rents his property to be used for distilleries,... Nor do we believe that any church should retain in its fellowship any member who drinks intoxicating liquors as a beverage....* [85]

A large part of society was arrayed alongside preachers against the use of alcohol. Interest was very high and evangelist Billy Sunday along with others who spoke to the subject drew very large crowds. The result was that laws on prohibition were passed, first in several individual states and then nationally in 1919, and consumption dramatically decreased.[86] There were also other beneficial results of Prohibition. During the Prohibition era (1919-1933), crime decreased 54%, the death rate due to liquor decreased 43%, 97 of the 98 Keeley Alcoholics Clinics closed for lack of patients, insanity decreased 66%, and all 60 Neil Cure Clinics closed for lack of patients afflicted with alcoholism.

> DURING THE PROHIBITION ERA (1919-1933):
> • Crime decreased 54%
> • The death rate, due to liquor, decreased 43%
> • 97 of the 98 Keeley Alcoholics Clinics closed for lack of patients
> • Insanity decreased 66%
> • All 60 Neil Cure Clinics closed for lack of patients afflicted with alcoholism

Contrary to popular opinion, Prohibition was quite successful. It didn't eradicate drinking, but it did significantly reduce consumption rates and thereby improve the public health. In his

---

[84] Lumpkins, *op.cit.*, p. 119.
[85] *Ibid*, p.31.
[86] http://www.renewamerica.com/columns/creech/051122 (Accessed 7/8/2011).

86

book *The Devaluing of America*, William Bennett, former director
of the Office of National Drug Control Policy under President
George H.W. Bush, said: "One of the clear lessons of Prohibition
is that when we had laws against alcohol there was less
consumption, less alcohol-related disease, fewer drunken brawls,
and a lot less drunkenness. Contrary to myth, there is no evidence
that Prohibition caused any big increases in crime.[87]

To recap, the early 1900's was a time when:
- ✓ the evil of drinking was well known in society;
- ✓ liberal church leaders endorsed it;
- ✓ evangelicals fought it, preached and taught extensively
  against it.

Societal and Christian attitudes toward alcoholic consumption from 1950 -- 1980

By 1950, Prohibition was a thing of the past: criticized, repealed and all but forgotten. Society was once more free to buy and consume alcohol, though there were still a few locations where prohibition was in force. One could easily purchase alcoholic beverages even in grocery stores. Massive television advertisement encouraging use of alcohol was just beginning, but its effect was dramatic. There was a surge in drinking, in alcohol abuse, in youth drinking, and in social acceptance of alcohol. In an article in *Times Magazine* (Nov. 5, 1979), the Dean of students at

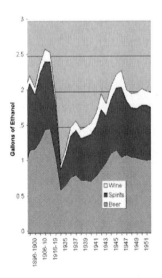

[87] *Ibid.*

Chicago's Loyola University was quoted as saying, "The single greatest drug abuse on this or any campus is undoubtedly alcohol."[88] The same article goes on to say,

- ✓ *"Some sample results [of a poll] at 34 New England four-year colleges show that more than 95% of the undergraduates report at least occasional drinking, compared with 59% who smoke marijuana, 11% who snort cocaine and 10% who pop tranquilizers.*

- ✓ *Twenty percent of the men and 10% of the women say getting drunk "was important" to them.*

- ✓ *The category of "heavy drinkers"—those who regularly consume more than a six-pack of beer or five shots of liquor at a sitting—now includes 29% of undergraduate men and 11% of the women.*

This terrible condition was only beginning to manifest itself in 1950, and the problem was full-blown by 1980.

There are two facts that came to light during this time: the fact that consumption of alcohol was beginning to be accepted by a significant portion of American society and the frightening fact that the evangelical churches in America had abandoned their role of warning society against this public menace.

A quote from a popular evangelist's book written in 1980 will illustrate the first fact. Quoted earlier in this chapter, he describes how a marriage that started so well went so drastically downhill due to alcohol abuse that the wife was desperate. This anecdote speaks of one particular case but is found to be true of hundreds of thousands of cases throughout society.

First they had enjoyed a few beers together.... "Nobody gets drunk on beer," he had said.... Before long, beer belonged. It was

---

[88] http://www.time.com/time/magazine/article/0,9171,912518,00.html#ixzz1QIBrCUjP, (Accessed 6/25/2011).

88

present for every evening... it became the drink to serve when friends dropped in.
When he had begun to climb in the company, there was entertaining to be done.... "Social drinking."
His drinking had increased....When he wanted to stop drinking, he couldn't.... She was sick of his drinking, of his lies, of his broken promises.[89]

The second fact, that the evangelical churches in America had abandoned their role of warning society, is harder to document since the "absence" of something is always hard to prove. It is clear, however, that evangelical leaders were not speaking out or writing on the subject. In 1950, as far as I can discover, there was not one single book on the market in America which proved that grape juice was in the Bible and that God did not condone moderate drinking. The only book dealing with the subject, out of print for a long time (since republished), was Rev William Patton's book, *Bible Wines or the Laws of Fermentation and Wines of the Ancients*. Robert Teachout's book, *Wine The Biblical Imperative: Total Abstinence*, based on a doctoral thesis, was published in 1983.

And yet, in 1950, evangelical churches were still living in the shadow of all the teaching and preaching of the proceeding era, and they almost universally lived and promoted abstinence. Most evangelical churches included in their church covenants a statement on this. Though there was little teaching on the central issue of the proper interpretation of the Bible words for grape juice and wine, there was an emphasis on purity and a consensus that alcohol and its effects were bad and a Christian should not partake. This consensus was not at all shared by the liberal denominations. The blessed fact that abstinence was the norm among evangelical churches was definitely the result of the battle for abstinence during the Prohibition and preceding eras. The tragic side of this "blessed fact" was that a standard of living was promoted

---

[89] Van Impe, Jack, *Alcohol The Beloved Enemy*, Thomas Nelson Publishers, Nashville, 1980; p. 19.

but there was no teaching to align it with the Bible. Maintaining a standard of abstinence without attaching it to biblical teaching led to either legalism or abandonment of the standard.

To recap, 1950 – 1980 was a time when:
- ✓ the evil of drinking was well known in society and increasing among youth;
- ✓ liberal church leaders endorsed it;
- ✓ some evangelical leaders began promoting moderate consumption;
- ✓ most evangelical churches still practiced abstinence;
- ✓ teaching that grape juice is in the Bible and that God condemned alcoholic beverages was almost unknown.

Societal and Christian attitudes toward alcoholic consumption in the early 2000's

An enormous change took place in evangelical churches by the year 2000. This change could be likened to a tsunami. Jaeggli says (citing a survey of nine evangelical liberal-arts colleges and seven seminaries): "In 1951, 98% of students in these institutions agreed that it was always wrong to drink Alcohol, but that percentage dropped to only  17% by 1982."[90] Undoubtedly, today the percentage would be even lower. Church leaders and Biblical scholars no longer warned about the dangers of alcohol. They began to write and to teach about the wrongness of abstinence and the Biblical reasons for moderate drinking. Even those who still espoused abstinence defended the one-wine theory of Bible interpretation and the resulting teaching that Jesus made and drank an alcoholic beverage. This teaching came at a time when society was becoming completely complacent about the sale and consumption of alcohol. While law enforcement agencies fought the

---

[90] Robert Jaeggli, *Christian and Drinking, a Biblical Perspective on Moderation and Abstinence* (Greenville, SC: BJU Press, 2008), p. 4

effects, drinking itself was universally accepted in society as a whole and more and more among Christians. How much society changed in just 50 years is amazing.

There are three specific changes that brought about the over-all transformation: the bombardment of advertising encouraging alcohol consumption, increased consumption of alcohol among the youth, and a continued shift in the attitude of most evangelical churches toward alcoholic beverages – the abandonment of abstinence. These changes will be considered at length in the following pages.

Bombardment of advertising encouraging alcohol consumption

By the year 2000 most Americans had color television and spent many hours watching it. This made the constant stream of advertising of

alcoholic products not only present in every home but made these products seem very innocuous, interesting, and enticing. Although society was now officially aware of the dangers of tobacco, there were no warnings attached to alcoholic products even though numerous studies showed the increased danger of alcohol consumption. It was always presented as an important and necessary part of social activities and a healthy and satisfying way to find happiness. Advertisers routinely promoted

health, fun, and sex with their advertisements which targeted youth.

This advertising blitz has advanced since 2000. Advertising companies are now searching for ways to invade the i-phones of the youth with advertisements of alcoholic beverages!

This advertising has resulted in a dramatic increase in sales of all alcoholic beverages, but it has perhaps caused the greatest increase in the sale of wine. One winery boasts "80  years ago we bottled MOONSHINE. Now we bottle sunshine!" The graphic on the increase of wineries in NC will show this increase.

Increased consumption of alcohol among the youth

In the introduction we quoted two shocking statistics:

- ✓ One quarter of American teenagers are into "binge drinking."
- ✓ By the age of 16 most kids will have seen 75,000 ads for alcohol. Young people view 20,000 commercials each year, and nearly 2,000 are for beer and wine.[91]

Does this advertising succeed? Very definitely -- if it did not, the producers would not pay the enormous cost for advertising their products. We do not have to wonder at its success; recent studies have documented it:

A study found that, among a group of 2,250 middle-school students in Los Angeles, those who viewed more television programs containing alcohol commercials while in the seventh grade were more likely in the eighth grade to drink beer,

---

[91] http://www.ecstasyaddiction.com/PressReleasePages/therealcostofalcoholadvertising.html (Accessed 8/8/2011).

wine/liquor, or to drink three or more drinks on at least one occasion during the month prior to the follow-up survey.

Researchers followed 3,111 students in S. Dakota from seventh to ninth grade, and found that exposure to in-store beer displays in grade 7 predicted onset of drinking by grade 9, and exposure to magazine advertising for alcohol at sports or music events predicted frequency of drinking in grade 9.[92]

When one thinks of the message of these commercials – fun and sex without limit – one can understand the appeal. The scary part of this is that the drinking problem is getting worse. With the demise of the church as a restraining factor there is nothing to inhibit the producers or the consumers. Liberal society is trying to take away legal restraints. As proof of this, you can google "Amethyst Initiative." I quote here from their web page:

Launched in July 2008, the Amethyst Initiative is made up of chancellors and presidents of universities and colleges across the United States. These higher education leaders have signed their names to a public statement that the problem of irresponsible drinking by young people continues despite the minimum legal drinking age of 21, and there is a culture of dangerous binge drinking on many campuses.

The Amethyst Initiative supports informed and unimpeded debate on the 21 year-old drinking age...[93]

In their statement, they declare that "It's time to rethink the drinking age [because] twenty-one is not working."[94] They want to lower it to 18.

---

[92] www.camy.org/factsheets/index.php?FactsheetID (Accessed 8/8/2011).

[93] http://www.amethystinitiative.org. (Accessed 6/28/2011).

[94] http://www.amethystinitiative.org/statement/ (Accessed 8/8/2011).

Even though there are still laws against underage drinking, consider this:

> *Not only did underage drinkers consume 11 percent of all alcoholic beverages purchased in the United States in 2002, but also the vast majority of the alcohol purchased for underage consumption was consumed in binge and heavy drinking.*[95]

A continued shift in the attitude of most evangelical churches toward alcoholic beverages, toward the abandonment of abstinence

It was mentioned in the introduction that Bible colleges are changing their teaching on the consumption of alcohol. By 1950 the teaching about the presence of grape juice in the Bible and God's condemnation of all alcoholic beverages had all but disappeared, though abstinence was still being taught and was found in most evangelical church constitutions. In the early 2000's there are voices being raised to actively promote moderate drinking in evangelical circles and to aggressively attack those who would continue to teach abstinence. Even those who do still stand for abstinence do not teach the position that not all "wine" in the Bible is alcoholic.

Since it would be a lengthy process to quote from so many leaders of the different denominations, the demonstration of the dramatic turn towards consumption of alcohol will be limited to the Southern Baptist Convention. This is because the SBC held to a position on abstinence longer than most other groups and because it is the largest group. Peter Lumpkins, a Southern Baptist minister and writer, has done much research on the recent change in the position of the SBC. He says concerning the historical position of the SBC,

> *Beginning in 1886 up until 2006, no fewer than 40 resolutions have been passed by Southern Baptists (Richard Land, 2008). All*

---

[95] Lumpkins, *op. cit.*, p. 21.

> *of these presumably presented the same message: total abstinence from alcoholic beverages for pleasurable purposes.*[96]

The following quotes about the present message of many SBC leaders are from his book, *Alcohol Today: Abstinence in an Age of Indulgence*:

> *The Christian Church (especially the Protestant side) that was virtually unanimous in support of the "old, failed Prohibition" policies will go on record quickly these days, if asked, that imbibing alcoholic beverages is not as bad as it used to be (p. 19).*

> *One professor from a Southern Baptist seminary had this to say: "Are alcoholic beverages a good thing? Sure. Within moderate amounts, of course. In fact don't ever let anyone tell you any differently. If they do, they are closet Roman Catholics who are imposing pharisaical legalism on you. They do not hold to Scripture." (p. 20).*

> *The idea that to drink a glass of wine, or any other alcoholic beverage, is a sin against God is so foreign to the teaching of the inspired, inerrant Word of God that for anyone to say to a Christian who has no conviction about drinking alcoholic beverages, 'You are sinning against God when you drink a glass of wine' is a sin itself. (p. 33, quoting president of Baptist General Convention of Oklahoma).*

> *The approaching crisis for Southern Baptists concerns behavior – a cataclysmal moral shift away from the biblical holiness expressed in biblical Lordship, toward the relativistic **postmodern** norms of American pop culture, including its hedonistic obsession with fulfilling desires. (p. 34,35).*[97]

Since the Southern Baptist Convention is the largest Baptist denomination in the world, the changes in their official position are

---

[96] Lumpkins, *op. cit.*, p. 31.

[97] Peter Lumpkins, *op cit.*

significant and reveal a trend that is probably even more advanced in all the rest of evangelical churches, though some still hold to abstinence.

To recap, societal and Christian attitudes toward alcoholic consumption by the early 2000's has evolved dramatically and that in just 50 years. It has been a time when:

- ✓ The evil of drinking alcohol has become accepted as normal in society and the youth lead the way in "pushing the envelope";
- ✓ liberal church leaders continue to endorse freedom to drink alcoholic beverages;
- ✓ many evangelical leaders promote moderate consumption of alcohol;
- ✓ other evangelicals neither fight it nor preach and teach against it;
- ✓ few evangelical churches practice abstinence aggressively;
- ✓ the teaching that grape juice is in the Bible is attacked by all but a very few.

XI.   Moderate Consumption of Alcohol

In chapter I it was mentioned that most of the Radio dramatizations of Pacific Garden Mission during the 1950's were stories of professional men with families who started out with light (or moderate) social drinking and then went on to become down-and-out bums on skid row where they found the Savior and gave up their alcohol. In Chapter X, I cited a story of a man who started with moderate drinking and went on to alcoholic dependence and a failing marriage. The fact is that very few people start drinking moderately with the goal of arriving at alcohol abuse, but that is often what happens.

Today there are a great many proponents of moderate drinking for health and other reasons, and many of its proponents are Christian leaders. Here we will discuss four elements of the question: "Should Christians start drinking alcohol moderately?" We will find that moderate drinking is not a healthy addition to a person's diet, that moderate drinking is dangerous, that moderate drinking can lead to serious consumption of alcoholic beverages, and that there are proponents of moderate drinking among Christian leaders in spite of the dangers.

Moderate drinking does not have health benefits

Here, we are questioning a very popular scientific "fact" repeated on the internet, in blogs, and other literature. We make the following statement on good authority and note that this is not a personal conclusion:

> *An Addiction Specialist and Senior Scientist at the Centre for Addiction and Mental Health at the University of Toronto states that "the health benefits of alcohol use are generally overstated and are virtually non-existent for young people. Even small amounts of alcohol increase*

*the risk of injury and boost the chances of deve-
loping about sixty diseases."⁹⁸*

The key here is that even IF there were health benefits we would say, "Watch out for the side effects. Watch out for the effects of the poison you would put in your body and its subsequent consequences."

But there is a simple and very scientific answer to all the promotion of wine as a simple health producer. The benefits are in the grape juice! An article put on the web by CNN Health reports:

If you don't like wine, the latest studies show you can get almost all the same benefits from grape juice. The reason [is that] purple grape juice contains the same powerful disease-fighting antioxidants, called flavonoids, that are believed to give wine many of its heart-friendly benefits.

What'll it be Wine or Welch's?

The flavonoids in grape juice, like those in wine, have been shown to prevent the oxidation of so-called bad cholesterol LDLs, or low-density lipoproteins that leads to formation of plaque in artery walls.

In a study published in 1999 in the journal Circulation, researchers at the University of Wisconsin Medical School in Madison asked 15 patients who already showed clinical signs of cardiovascular disease including plaque-constricted arteries to drink a tall glass of grape juice daily. After 14 days, blood tests revealed that LDL oxidation in these patients was significantly reduced. And ultrasound images showed changes in the artery walls, indicating that their blood was flowing more freely.

Grape juice can also lower the risk of developing the blood clots that lead to heart attacks, according to unpublished findings from

⁹⁸ Rehn, Jurgen, et al. *Alcohol as Damaging as Tobacco.* Nature. April 8, 2004. Quoted by MA Department of Public Health. Report reproduced in Appendix II.

Georgetown University researcher Jane Freedman, M.D. So can red wine, but in this case grape juice is the more practical way to go. Wine only prevents blood from clotting when it's consumed at levels high enough to declare someone legally drunk, says University of Wisconsin researcher John Folts, Ph.D. With grape juice, you can drink enough to get the benefit without worrying about becoming intoxicated.[99]

Moderate drinking is dangerous

There are those in society and especially in law enforcement who are very much aware of the dangers of moderate drinking. This awareness has been in existence for a very long time. A statement in a School Physiology Journal in 1900 states:

I affirm that a man who abstains totally from the use of alcoholic drinks does not deny himself anything; he gains in the blessing and joy of life. No drunkard, was ever saved by the resolution to become a moderate drinker. Salvation consists in avoiding the first glass. The moderate drinker tempts others. It is not the drunkards who lead men astray; they rather have the great merit of deterring others by their example.

> *The moderate drinker tempts others.*

Those who lead others into temptation are the moderate drinkers. And so long as this temptation continues there will be no end to intemperance and its results, namely, disease, insanity, and crime. Whoever fails to recognize this fact does not understand the history of the warfare against intemperance.

In modern times we can be more technical. Here are some statements by the Mayo Clinic and the AMA:

---

[99] http://articles.cnn.com/2000-03-31/health/wine.heart.wmd_1_grape-juice-nonalcoholic-wine-john-folts?_s=PM:HEALTH. Accessed 9/22/2011.

Alcohol use is a slippery slope. Moderate drinking can offer some health benefits. But it's easy to drink too heavily, leading to serious health consequences.[100]

The American Medical Association issued a report yesterday showing that adolescents and young adults who drink alcohol may risk long-lasting brain damage, particularly related to learning, memory and critical thinking. The report is a synthesis of nearly two decades of research on alcohol and the brain.

While individuals may joke about killing brain cells as they guzzle their beers, the research suggests that even as little as a few beers can actually cause harm.[101]

The Massachusetts government in a report about moderate drinking says:

➤ *According to the World Health Organization, "there may be some danger that talking about a 'safe limit' (for alcohol use) will encourage more of the population to drink and spur light drinkers to drink up to the stated limit."*

➤ *Moderate drinking levels are generally defined as no more than one drink per day for women (under age 65) and no more than two drinks per day for men (under 65). These limits are based on differences between the sexes in both weight and metabolism.*

➤ *Elderly (above age 65) should limit alcohol intake because their bodies process alcohol differently. The maximum limits of drinks a day for men over 65 is 1 drink per day, and for women over 65 is less than one per day.*

➤ *There are no safe limits for alcohol use by youth.[102]*

[100] http://www.mayoclinic.com/health/alcohol/SC00024, (Accessed 6/28/2011).
[101] http://www.unm.edu/~cosap/RESEARCH.HTM, (Accessed 6/28/2011).

Moderate drinking can lead to serious consumption of alcoholic beverages

The same report made other pertinent statements:

> ➤ *"In addition to the potential individual consequences of increased alcohol consumption, the public may suffer from the promotion of moderate drinking."*

> ➤ *"Although drinking is a personal act and an individual responsibility, it is also behavior shaped by our societies and something for which society as a whole has responsibility."*

> ➤ *According to the World Health Organization, "measures that influence drinkers in general will also have an impact on heavier drinkers. Promoting increased levels of moderate drinking may in turn increase overall consumption, even for those who should not do so."*[103]

The government defines moderate drinking as "one drink per day for women and two drinks per day for men." This becomes vital if one exceeds permitted levels of alcohol in the blood since most states now have very severe penalties for driving under the influence. At this point we need to be very clear what moderate drinking is for a Christian.

What is moderate drinking by Bible standards? We are constantly reminded by those who teach the one-wine theory that wine in the Bible had a much lower alcohol content than today's alcoholic beverages.

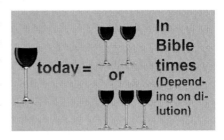

---

[102] www.mass.gov/...**abuse**/prevention_advice_moderate_drinking_safe.rtf (Accessed 6/28/2011). This entire interesting report is included with permission in Appendix II.
[103] *Ibid.*

Actually, without going through the mathematical equations necessary, we can say that just one glass of wine today has the alcohol equivalent of two or three glasses in Bible times.

When we look at the **effects** of moderate drinking, the dangers worsen. First, "one more for the road" is not a wise choice. The news reports are constantly assailing us with tragedies that happen suddenly after the faculties have been impaired by alcohol.

Secondly, the influence of moderate social drinking on families is very great. When children are taught by their parents' example that a "celebration" requires alcohol for the adults or that a full meal requires alcohol for the parents, children develop a desire to be able to one day partake in that adult activity. Of

course if they are permitted to taste the alcohol at the table, it becomes just that much worse. They are totally unprotected the first time they are offered alcohol in an unsupervised situation.

Proponents of moderate drinking among Christian leaders

In spite of the well-known dangers of moderate drinking, there are an increasing number of Christians who forcefully defend it. The default view of the Church today about the recreational consumption of intoxicating beverages, according to Peter Lumpkins, is **moderation.** He says that the mantra is very clear and memorable: *The Bible*

102

condemns the abuse of intoxicating drink, not the use of intoxicating drink.[104]

A blog on moderate drinking sums up the attitude of many:

> *Drinking socially -- not "getting drunk" -- can be an opportunity to demonstrate the Gospel message. Christians who drink with restraint show that they're strong enough in their faith to be controlled by God and not be slaves to alcohol, food or other worldly desires.*

> *Plus, it gives them an opportunity to share their message in settings where drinking is the norm, without coming off like a Bible-thumping teetotaler. A story I wrote about a young (hip, even) church in Chicago started this way: "A pastor walks into a bar."*

> *No, this isn't a joke; it's a new scene for American Christianity: Young guys in their 20s and 30s forming Christian communities in pubs, concert halls, cafes and art galleries.*

> *..."We want a church that reflects the city of Chicago and the neighborhoods we're in," said Pastor Mark Bergrin. "I want to reach the guys at the pub across the street from me."*

> *Christian groups across the spectrum, from Catholics to non-denominational congregations, have started new ministries to bring together beer and the Bible, to put "theology on tap." They're meeting in bars, serving booze at Bible study and inserting their message into places where communities are already forming, reaching people where they are rather than forcing them into a church building.*[105]

---

[104] Lumpkins, *op. cit.*, p. 81.
[105] *http://blog.chron.com/believeitornot/2010/07/pour-one-for-the-pastor-evangelical-perspectives-on-alcohol-and-the-church/* (Accessed 6/28/2011).

This is a view with growing popularity, and those who try to combat it are often reviled.

Most Christian leaders who espouse moderate drinking for Christians today are using Scripture to defend their thesis. Most of these Christian leaders will also say that a proper drink in Bible times was always greatly diluted. However, one drink today already has the alcoholic content of 2 or 3 drinks in Bible times, leading to the conclusion that the Bible cannot support the moderate drinking of today.

This brings us back to the question: "Should Christians start drinking alcohol moderately?" If one chooses to ignore the dangers and teach one's children to do likewise, one will advance in the direction of moderate drinking. If one wants to take seriously the dangers of alcohol and the admonitions of the Lord, one will abstain and teach his children to do likewise.

XII.   The Importance of Abstinence for the Christian

Beyond the questions concerning the interpretation of God's Word, there is a very important matter of application. Over seventy-five years ago there was a turning away from that interpretation which affirmed the actuality of grape juice in the Bible to that which mandated only alcohol. Some modern writers continue this "belief" and enlarge it to affirm that in Bible times those who pleased God drank "moderately," so Christians may drink moderately today. Yet, some of them feel that it is best to abstain altogether.

Many who do believe in moderation say that we must warn people to be moderate, but we must be careful not to speak too much about the dangers of alcoholic beverages so as not to offend anyone. These same Christians would never moderately react if their child were running out into the street. They would never moderately wake their family up if their house were on fire! And yet they will teach their children that they can drink moderately of a product which is deliberately produced to attack the powers of judgment.

It is often considered that "moderate" means only one glass of an alcoholic beverage, but this would mean that a person is always just one glass removed from going beyond moderate. It seems that wisdom itself demands that we not even take the risk of trying to keep it "under control." Consider the authoritative and inspired wisdom of Proverbs 23:31-33: *"Look not thou upon the wine when it is red, when it giveth his colour in the cup, when it moveth itself aright. At the last it biteth like a serpent, and stingeth like an adder."* Going against this Scriptural warning, whoever practices "moderate drinking" and tries to not go beyond puts himself unwisely within reach of getting bit by the "serpent-like" wine.

Christians need to speak out concerning the dangers of alcoholic beverages. Author Jim McGuiggan says *"even in small amounts it affects speech and balance and impairs judgment."*[106] He goes on to quote a scientist who discusses drinking and driving: "The drinker is in the worst possible position to make the decision whether he is safe to drive or not.... Alcohol is detectable in the brain within a half a minute after being swallowed...." In fact, the drinker is in no position to make any moral decisions. A Christian should never be in such a position (see 1 Peter 1:13; 4:7; 5:8; Titus 2:6).

Those who teach their children to drink moderately leave them totally unprotected when they go out with friends who do not drink moderately. Look at these statistics:

1. *The average age at which Americans begin drinking regularly is 15.9 years old.*

2. *Teens that begin drinking before age 15 are 5 times more likely to develop alcohol dependence than those who begin drinking at age 21.*

3. *An early age of drinking onset is also associated with alcohol-related violence not only among persons under age 21 but among adults as well.*[107]

The same web page quotes Joseph A. Califano Jr., Chairman and President of the National Center on Addiction and Substance Abuse at Columbia University as saying: *"A child who reaches age 21 without smoking, abusing alcohol or using drugs is virtually certain never to do so."*

Actually, in discussing the dangers of alcohol, we must go even further. Many Christians are aware of the danger of becoming an alcoholic. It has often been said that taking a drink of an alcoholic

[106] *Ibid.*
[107] *Focus Adolescent Services*, http://www.focusas.com/Alcohol.html (accessed: 8/5/2009).

106

beverage is like playing Russian roulette because one doesn't know if he will become addicted or not.

Many do not realize that there is the danger of alcohol abuse[108] for all who drink moderately. A recent television show on the health channel gave the three top causes of death in the USA: smoking, obesity, and alcohol abuse (not alcoholism). Alcohol abuse leads to disease, accidents, and crimes which stem from any use of alcohol. The dramatic difference between these three is that those who indulge in obesity and smoking essentially only harm themselves–that is bad enough! – but alcohol abuse is often the direct cause of death and suffering for totally innocent persons.

> ...alcohol abuse is a pattern of drinking that can result in physical injury; ongoing alcohol-related relationship problems; the failure to attend to important responsibilities at school, work, or at home; and/or the experience of recurring alcohol-related legal problems (such as receiving multiple DWIs and DUIs) during a twelve-month time period.[109]

The extreme danger of alcohol abuse is that it does not take a regular pattern of drinking to be lethal. Just one episode is enough to ruin many lives. Consider a high school student who has been taught that drinking in itself is not wrong. Then he finds himself with the wrong friends, has just three drinks, and has a fatal accident on the way home.

While the whole world would be sad at such a tragedy, it would not change the bent on encouraging the alcohol industry which has rendered itself, in fact, accomplice by piously calling for moderation, all the while setting the stage for many more such tragedies. While I do not expect better from the world, I do from those who claim belief in Christ.

---

[108] See Appendix 3 for the difference between *alcohol abuse* and **alcoholism**.
[109] http://www.about-alcohol-abuse.com. (accessed on 01/07/10).

Sadly, all too often, there is in our churches a pervasive silence on these problems and what the Bible says about "wine." Any subject addressed so frequently in the Bible, such as the dangers of alcohol consumption, deserves mention and study.

Even if Christians disagree about the meaning of the word "wine" in the Bible, they should be willing to consider the dangers of alcohol. At least Charles Spurgeon, though he personally believed that drinking alcoholic beverages moderately was permitted for Christians and for himself, gave it up in order not to be a stumbling block. When we realize the terrible danger of parents teaching their children that drinking alcohol is blessed by God, it would seem that such parents should consider changing their lifestyle to protect their children. In Romans 14, the apostle Paul discussed the principle of a "strong" brother giving up what he considered to be permissable (eating meat sacrificed to idols), in order not to cause the fall of someone who thought that this would be wrong. He also said in 1 Corinthians 8:13: "Wherefore, if meat make my brother to offend, I will eat no flesh while the world standeth, lest I make my brother to offend."

Peter Masters wrote a book, *Should Christians Drink?* His answer is a resounding "no"!

> *We should shudder that the world has taken alcohol and made it such a force for destruction, misery and horror.*

> *We should shudder at the way it subdues the higher senses even of the countless men and women who drink only moderately.*

> *We should shudder away from a product which causes an estimated 10 to 16 million children under eighteen to have to grow up in the living nightmare of a shattered alcoholic home.*

> *We should shudder that the greatest component of the human frame -- the rational faculty -- is regularly blurred and distorted*

108

by alcohol, so that the baser part of the human nature is released.[110]

We need to go beyond this principle of being willing to give up what one believes to be right.

The EVIDENCE presented in this book that grape juice is present in the Bible and that God never blesses the consumption of alcohol cannot be ignored. This evidence must be presented to give Christians confidence that God does not condone the drinking of alcoholic beverages in any form. Pastors and Bible scholars must fearlessly teach on this subject. Paul said: *"Wherefore I take you to record this day, that I am pure from the blood of all men. For I have not shunned to declare unto you all the counsel of God"* (Acts 20:26,27).

---

[110] Masters, Peter, *Should Christians Drink.*

Conclusion

This book is the result of my search for the truth concerning the presence of grape juice in the Bible. Certain experiences in my life and regular Bible reading made me question current teaching on the subject. When I realized that my personal belief was wrong and that there were many proofs of grape juice in the Bible, I was pressed to write this book to help other Christians know the truth and take a stand against alcohol.

To present these proofs, we made this study follow the same logic as my own studies. We had to consider the challenge that God seems to be inconsistent or to contradict Himself in His usage of the word "wine" in Scripture. We saw that God blessed Israel and their "wine." He said: *"And he will love thee, and bless thee, and multiply thee: he will also __bless__ the fruit of thy womb, and the fruit of thy land, thy corn, and thy wine and thine oil..."* (Deuteronomy 7:13). This promise was kept according to 1Ki 4:25: *" And Judah and Israel dwelt safely, every man under his vine and under his fig tree, from Dan even to Beersheba, all the days of Solomon."* In the Bible, nothing pictured God's blessing better than the vine. He created it to produce healthy grape juice; He promised it, planned for it, and provided it in the Promised Land to give His people gladness of heart (Psalms 104:14,15).

And yet, God also said about "wine" in the Bible: *"Woe unto them that rise up early in the morning, that they may follow strong drink; that continue until night, till wine inflames them"* (Isaiah 5:11). A little further, Isaiah says: *"Woe unto them that are mighty to drink wine..."* (v. 22). These verses effectively show that there were people in Israel who drank "wine" made from the vine and that God condemned this act. God not only condemned drinking "wine," but He promised judgment to Israel for misusing the fruit of the vine. Hosea says (7:1-13): *"the iniquity of Ephraim was discovered... they commit falsehood... they are all adulterers... have made him sick with bottles of wine... they do not return to the LORD their God, nor seek him for all this. Woe unto them! For they have fled from me: destruction unto them! Because they have transgressed against me."* Being "sick with wine" is an important transgression!

Next we continued our study with the meaning of the word wine in Scripture. We determined that there are several Hebrew words used for the product of the vine and for other beverages. These words were translated by one Greek word *"oinos"* and by one English word *"wine."* Because of this, we can conclude that, in Greek and in English, the word used is generic (not specific). The assumption that the word is specific has led to the confusion about God's blessing and condemning the same product. Studying the Hebrew words helps clear up the confusion. Even with just the English translation, God has been very consistent in giving enough background and context in each use of the word "wine" to permit us to understand why He sometimes blesses the fruit of the vine and at other times curses its use. I believe His condemnation and warning against the product have everything to do with when it has been tainted with what causes intoxication (i.e. alcoholic wine). In contrast, I believe His blessing and encouragement have everything to do with the proper use of the product when it is kept unadulterated and used in a way that poses no risk of rendering someone less sober (i.e. grape juice). Therefore, we can say that, depending on the context, often the same word in English is used for what amounts to be two very different substances: alcoholic beverages and unfermented grape juice.

To give us a better perspective on the problem, we studied the historical development of Christian attitudes toward alcohol in our country by briefly looking at the Temperance Movement in Chapter VI.

We continued our search for the truth by going deeper into the study of just how important truth is to God, and how necessary it is for us to understand it as it comes from Him. This led us to a consideration of the necessity of "rightly dividing" or interpreting God's Word. We found that proper, historical methods of interpretation are absolutely essential to a proper understanding of Biblical truth.

Applying these methods helped us conclude that the Bible does indeed speak much of grape juice. Also the application of these methods helped us answer the question: Did Jesus make and drink alcoholic wine? Jesus, the creator of the universe and the holy Son of God, did **not** make an alcoholic beverage and give it to those who had already "well drunk." He obeyed God's laws unfailingly and from water created refreshingly delicious grape juice for His friends. Jesus, God's perfect sacrifice for sin, did not drink an alcoholic beverage during the Passover Supper. He fulfilled all of God's qualifications for a perfect sacrifice. He partook only of products that had no leaven in them: unleavened bread and unfermented juice, "the fruit of the vine." This point is very important because it removes the primary excuse that Christians use to permit them to consume alcoholic beverages.

The fact of grape juice in the Bible allows us to recognize and affirm that God is consistent in Himself and in His Word. We can state with confidence that He blesses the fruit of the vine, grape juice, and He condemns the use of alcoholic wine. At last, it can be said that God blessed Israel and their <u>grape juice</u> when He said in Deut. 7:13: *"And he will love thee, and bless thee, and multiply thee: he will also bless the fruit of thy womb, and the fruit of thy land, thy corn, and thy <u>grape juice</u>, and thine oil, the increase of thy kine, and the flocks of thy sheep, in the land which he sware unto thy fathers to give thee."* He also said in Isaiah 55:1: *"Ho, every one that thirsteth, come ye to the waters, and he that hath no money; come ye, buy, and eat; yea, come, buy <u>grape juice</u> and milk without money and without price."*

We can also state with authority that God condemned the use of alcoholic wine when He said: *"Woe unto them that rise up early in the morning, that they may follow strong drink; that continue until night, till (alcoholic) wine inflame them"* (Isaiah 5:11) and later in the same chapter, *"Woe unto them that are mighty to drink (alcoholic) wine..."* (Is. 5:22).

Thus we arrive at the necessary conclusion:

1. In the Bible, God repeatedly blesses and encourages the use of grape juice.
2. In the Bible, God repeatedly condemns the use of alcoholic wine in the strongest terms.
3. Modern Christians should **not** drink alcoholic beverages – even moderately.

Refusing to believe the presence of grape juice in Scripture is to admit that Christians today have every right to drink alcohol moderately. However, our study in Chapters IX through XI has proved that there is a growing problem with alcohol and that diluting wine or drinking moderately is not the answer. To say that God can bless and curse the same product, depending only on how much one partakes of the product, subtly and gravely implies that God condones or even encourages "playing with fire." To the contrary! God condemns even approaching a product that leads to saying perverse things (Proverbs 23:31-33), because it opens the way to temptation. This condemnation is the only act that would be consistent with God's thrice holy and good nature.

Those who would accept the wrong interpretation of Scripture (that God blesses alcoholic beverages) have grossly misunderstood Him. A bad interpretation of Scripture regarding wine ultimately will lead to maligning God's character -- a very serious offense! A Christian should never accept an understanding of God's Word that makes God contradict Himself. This is the real issue: God cannot contradict Himself.

Let us accept that God always speaks clearly and truly about what He expects His creatures to do. He tells us specifically Titus 2:12 that He wants us *"to live soberly, righteously, and godly in this present world..."*. As believers, we are called *"the salt of the earth"* (Mat. 5:13). Far from shying away from the subject of grape juice and wine in the Bible, we ought to address the subject with confidence and boldness. We who believe God's Word must be eager to see, understand, and share with others what He says in His Word, for God speaks clearly:

> *Love not the world, neither the things that are in the world. If any man love the world, the love of the Father is not in him* (1 John 2:15);

> *The Lord gave the word: great was the company of those that published it.* (Ps 68:11).

Appendix I

Was Jesus a Brewer

May 24, 2008 by John Moss[111]

I hope to study with you about the existence and nature of two different kinds of wine, fermented and unfermented. I will be drawing information from the old and new testaments, as well as historical accounts from ancient historians and explorers. We will look to see what type of wine Christ created at the wedding feast, what kind of wine was at the last supper, what wines were a blessing, and what wines were a curse.

Why many believe wine always means alcohol? Some of the blame is on the English language, some is on our culture. Palestine and southeastern Europe do not have the same habits regarding fermented or unfermented drink as northern Europe does. Many of us could trace our lineage back to German, English, Irish, or Scottish roots. These were (and are) peoples that frequently use strong drink on a daily basis. Those of us who are not from that lineage are still influenced by this, however. That, together with the fact that the King James Version (and all versions since then) have been translated in a culture where drinking alcoholic drinks was almost universally accepted, have given birth to what some have called the "One Wine Theory." That is, the belief that when wine is mentioned in the bible that it always means fermented grape juice. The main reason we make this mistake is that we judge the practices of ancient Palestine to be the same as ours. This is simply not the case. Half a world and two millennia away, we are far

---

[111] www.associatedcontent.com/article/784631/ was_jesus_abrewer.html?single page=true&cat=22 (used by permission of author).

removed from their way of life. So let's turn to history to find the truth of the matter.

Practices of the Ancients

To really understand the usage of the word "wine" in the Bible, we must look to the ancient practices of production of wine. This is an important topic to cover, since the prevailing modern belief is that there was no way to preserve perishable items before refrigeration, and hence there was no way to preserve grape juice unfermented in biblical times, therefore it must have all been alcoholic. This is not true, and there was in those days a precise science of ways to prevent unfermented grape juice from spoiling.

For fermentation to occur, a specific balance must exist between the leaven (or gluten), the amount of sugar (which itself becomes the alcohol), the texture or consistency of the liquid, and the temperature.

Production - 4 major ways to prevent the fermentation of grape juice

1. Boiling: By evaporating most of the water, the consistency is made into a syrup, and the sugar content is too high a ratio. For these reasons, it will not ferment.

> a. Herman Boerhave (born in 1668, author of *Elements of Chemistry*) states, "By boiling, the juice of the richest grapes loses all its aptitude for fermentation, and may afterwards be preserved for years without undergoing any further change."

> b. Parkinson, in his *Theatrum Batanicum* states "The juice or liquor pressed out of the ripe grapes is called *vinum* (Latin for wine). Of it are made both *sapa* and *defrutum*, in English that is to say "boiled wine" the latter boiled down to

the half, the former to the third." Here we can note that this boiled grape juice is still referred to as wine.

c. Aristotle, born in 384 BC says "The wine of Arcadia was so thick that it was necessary to scrape it from the skin bottles in which it was contained, and to dissolve the scrapings in water." Again we have this unfermented grape juice being referred to as wine.

d. The Mishna, a Jewish text, states that it was common practice of the Jews to drink boiled wine.

e. Dr. Eli Smith, an American missionary in Syria in 1846 wrote in his Bibliothecra Sacra "Of the vineyards, an unbroken space 2 miles long by half a mile wide only a few gallons of intoxicating wine are made. The wine made is an item of no consideration. It is not the most important, but rather the least so, of all the reasons the vine is cultivated." He goes on to confirm that the only form in which the unfermented grape juice is preserved is that of "dibbs," which may also be called grape-molasses. This is essentially the same process as has been used since Jesus's time in that region.

f. As a side note, the boiling point for grape juice is 212 degrees, but the point at which alcohol evaporates is 170 degrees, so even if some of it had fermented prior to being boiled, this would remove the alcohol.

2. Filtration: By filtering out the yeast, or leaven, from the grape juice one may prevent fermentation. The historian Plutarch writes *Wine is rendered old and feeble in strength when frequently filtered. The strength or spirit being thus excluded, the wine neither inflames the brain neither infests the mind and the passions, and is much more pleasant to drink.*

3. Subsidence: By allowing the leaven to settle, then pouring off the juice remaining, the gluten (another word for leaven or yeast) can be removed.

4. Fumigation: By introducing small amounts of sulphur into the juice, or into the container, fermentation can be prevented. One simple way of doing this is to add a small amount of chicken eggs to the mixture.

Biblical Wine

Sometimes word studies lend us additional understanding into the meaning of the Scripture, but unfortunately not so with this topic. The words Yayin (Hebrew) and Oinos (Greek) both are generic terms meaning simply "wine," not specifying whether the drink has alcohol. Modern examples would be the way we use the word cider. It can mean alcoholic cider or non-alcoholic. Also the word milk can mean many different types of milk, and in the South at least, asking for a coke will sometimes get the response "which kind." Similarly the words Yayin and Oinos themselves make no distinction between fermented or unfermented wine, but include both. So we have to look at the words in their context to determine their meaning. Also the Hebrew word "shakar" is often misunderstood. The translation is "strong drink," but in our modern practices we take that to mean "strong, intoxicating drink," as is our modern practice with distillation of liquor. However, distillation to create the "strong" liquor we know of today did not even exist until the 9th century. So this does not make sense with the Old Testament writing taking place over 1000 years earlier. Its meaning in that time actually meant wine made from fruits other than grapes, like dates, and mixed with honey and spices. This word is used generally, as is Yayin to mean either fermented or unfermented. Let's look at places where yayin is rendered wine, first at intoxicating wine, then at unintoxicating.

2 Sam: 13:28 "Now Absalom had commanded his servants, saying, Mark ye now when Amnon's heart is merry with wine, and when I say unto you, Smite Amnon; then kill him, fear not: have I not commanded you. Be courageous and be valiant."

Esther 1:10 "On the seventh day, when the heart of the king was merry with wine "

Now unintoxicating [wine in the following verses], and it is important to note that most of the meaning here must be derived from context.

Isa 16:10 *"And gladness is taken away, and joy out of the plentiful field, and in the vineyards there shall be no singing, neither shall there be shouting, the treaders shall tread out no wine in their presses, I have made their vintage shouting to cease."* The important part here is that Isaiah writes that what the treaders are treading out is wine. Naturally, this would be grape juice as it is coming fresh out of grapes.

Jer. 40:10, 12 *"As for me, behold, I will dwell at Mizpah to serve the Chaldeans, which will come unto us, but ye, gather ye wine, and summer fruits, and oil, and put them in your vessels, and dwell in your cities that ye have taken." "Even all the Jews returned out of all places whither they were driven, and came to the land of Judah, to Gedaliah unto Mizpah, and gathered wine and summer fruits very much."* Here again we see wine being used to refer to the natural product of a grape. One cannot gather alcoholic wine from a field but one can gather grapes. Fermentation is a time-controlled process.

Gen 49:11 *"Binding his foal unto the vine, and his ass's colt unto the choice vine, he washed his garments in wine, and his clothes in the blood of grapes."* Here you have parallelism, two statements that mean the same thing. Were not his clothes also his garments, and his garments clothes? The "blood of the grape" is clearly grape juice, as it is the natural juice of the grape. Because the statements are parallel, wine in this passage also means grape juice.

Now let's look at the New Testament, for the word Oinos, translated "wine." As before, we'll look at intoxicating and unintoxicating wine as well as how fermented wine is used as symbol for God's wrath.

Eph 5:18 *"And be not drunk with wine, wherein is excess; but be filled with the Spirit."*

To show unfermented grape juice, let's look at the "new wine in old bottles" Scripture in Matt 9:17, *"Neither do men put new wine into old bottles: else the bottles break, and the wine runneth out, and the bottles perish: but they put new wine into new bottles, and both are preserved."*

Corresponding Scriptures can be found in Mark 2:22 and Luke 5:37-38. Often times we hear from conventional wisdom, "Well, the wine was put into the new bottles because the old bottles could not handle the pressure." That is, the pressure caused by fermentation. The truth is, no animal skin could withstand that pressure, because not even thick glass bottles withstand it, and will shatter, if grape juice ferments within them. The practice was quite the opposite. Putting into new bottles was to prevent the juice from coming into contact with any possible fermenting agent in the old bottle, to prevent the process from occurring. Because if it did occur, the bottle would burst. Hence the old bottle bursting in this Scripture. This reinforces the idea that wine is also grape juice in some passages, and this translation fits the Scripture.

Rev 14:10 *"unmixed, undiluted or unweakened"*

Rev 16:19 God's wrath as a cup of wine, intoxicating and maddening to those forced to drink it.

Rev 17:1, 2

Water into Wine, and the communion

Now let's look at two major events that have wine associated with them, and determine the nature of wine used. First, let's talk about Jesus' miracle of turning water into wine. John 2:1-11:

> *And the third day there was a marriage in Cana of Galilee; and the mother of Jesus was there: And both Jesus was called, and his disciples, to the marriage. And when they wanted wine, the mother of Jesus saith unto him, They have no wine. Jesus saith unto her, Woman, what have I to do with thee? mine hour is not yet come. His mother saith unto the servants, Whatsoever he saith unto you, do it. And there were set there six waterpots of stone, after the manner of the purifying of the Jews, containing two or three firkins apiece. Jesus saith unto them, Fill the waterpots with water. And they filled them up to the brim. And he saith unto them, Draw out now, and bear unto the governor of the feast. And they bare it. When the ruler of the feast had tasted the water that was made wine, and knew not whence it was: (but the servants which drew the water knew;) the governor of the feast called the bridegroom, And saith unto him, Every man at the beginning doth set forth good wine; and when men have well drunk, then that which is worse: but thou hast kept the good wine until now. This beginning of miracles did Jesus in Cana of Galilee, and manifested forth his glory; and his disciples believed on him.*

This passage of Scripture has been used by many to justify drinking, as they will say "Jesus was a brewer." First of all, the wine at a Jewish wedding as indicated by the Mishnah and later the Talmud (Jewish texts) was to be non-alcoholic. It is well-known among Jews that leaven (yeast for example, whether added or naturally occurring, one of which is present in any fermentation) of any kind was forbidden at holy occasions, including marriage ceremonies.

Here we have to ask, "Which kind of wine would have fit Jesus's character?" For those that would contend that the wine was alcoholic, if Jesus made water into wine he would be promoting excess and debauchery. Eph 5:18 speaks against this. This is no small amount, anywhere from 18 to 27 gallons of water was made wine (two to three firkins). This would have violated Habakkuk 2:15! *Woe unto him that giveth his neighbour drink, that puttest thy bottle to him, and makes him drunken also, that thou mayest look on their nakedness!* By believing that this wine was intoxicating, we would be, in effect, destroying Christ's moral character. Through inspiration many times fermented wine is said to be "like an asp," a "mocker," and is even used to symbolize God's divine wrath. And Christ, being the Son of God, surely knew the terrible acts that people do when inebriated, and the path of destruction they might walk down. Would the Christ you know have given these people alcohol, knowing full well its effects? I think in that light, it is clear he did not. Wine here was clearly grape juice.

Now, let's examine the institution of the Lord's Supper, and see whether the drink here was alcoholic or not. Matt 26:27-29 First, we have to realize again the way things were done by the Jews in that day. Remember, leaven was strictly forbidden. That is the same reason we use unleavened bread, because that was what was certainly used in the original example. Since leaven is a critical component of fermentation, drinking alcoholic wine would violate the Jewish tradition and God's instructions for the Jews. Many Jews, in order to obey God's command, would press fresh grapes out into cups or pitchers themselves just prior to consumption to make certain that the juice was not fermented.

What is strange is that there should not even be any contention about the Lord's Supper. The Greek word "oinos" that is the generic word for wine is not even used here. The word used translates literally the fruit of the vine. No fermentation reference at all. Not even the possibility.

Again, if this had been alcohol Jesus would have violated Habbakuk 2:15, and would have violated the "no-leaven" rule of Passover. So certainly this was grape juice, without a doubt.

Some other verses for your own study about this topic:

Prov 23:20-21; Prov 23:29-35; Prov 20:1; Isa 28:7; Isa 5:22; Lev 10:9.

1 Timothy 5:23 *Drink no longer water, but use a little wine for thy stomach's sake and thine often infirmities.*

Here is one of the big Scriptures that people use to justify social drinking or drinking in moderation. Others use it for medicinal purposes. For one thing, there is a good chance this was non-alcoholic wine. But even if it was alcoholic, let us consider something. Before the discovery of distillation in the 9th Century, that is, using the old ways of making alcohol, wine would usually have about a 3% alcohol content. That's less than a modern day beer. Note this Scripture can also be rendered "drink no longer water only" or "drink no longer water exclusively." This could mean that he still drank water sometimes, and wine sometimes, or even mixed the two. Modern-day wine has anywhere from 11-20% alcohol. To achieve the same alcohol level one would have to water the wine down heavily. Personally, I think it is just as likely that here again wine means only grape juice (oinos is used); however, there is not sufficient context to determine for certain.

Modern science has discovered that grape juice has many health benefits that wine does, and in some ways is actually better. To quote from CNN's website, "*Purple grape juice contains the same powerful disease-fighting antioxidants, called flavonoids, that are believed to give wine many of its heart-friendly benefits.*" and further, "*the antioxidants in grape juice appear to linger in the body longer than do those in wine.*"

As a side note, the source went on to say that the same level of health benefit could not come from eating table grapes, because the juice is made from pressing the skin and seeds as well, and many table grapes are seedless. Also, red or "purple" grapes are used here, the white variety is much weaker with respect to health benefits. In conclusion, I hope that I have shown to you sufficient proof to convince you that there were two different types of wines spoken of in the Bible, and that though one is only grape juice and counted as a blessing in many Scriptures, the other is alcoholic, and is the cause of many types of violence, strife, disobedience, and is even the symbol of God's wrath in Revelation. Consider for yourself the kind of example we would set for our families and our communities.

Finally, as a disclaimer, I have used King James Version verses here, but I think you will find they differ little in their essential meaning in other generally accepted translations. We may not always agree with one another on issues, but I hope what I have written will at least be somewhat educational. All entries have been considered to the best of my abilities, and the passages of scripture transcribed as carefully as possible. If you feel talkative, please leave a comment. I appreciate it.

124

Appendix II

Is Moderate Drinking Really Safe Drinking?

MA Department of Public Health[112]

Adults are advised to be cautious when consuming alcohol and consider their personal situation before deciding to drink. Contacting your health care provider before changing drinking patterns can help to prevent problems. Remember that a healthy diet, avoidance of smoking, and maintenance of an appropriate level of physical activity and weight can help to maintain a strong heart, as well as enhance one's outlook.

Recent Reports

The Bureau of Substance Abuse Services cautions Massachusetts residents to consider their personal circumstance as well as the potential for negative effects before consuming alcohol.

Studies may show that "light or moderate drinkers have lower rates of coronary heart disease than abstainers." Yet this doesn't tell the whole story.[113]

Facts to Consider

- Factors such as a healthy diet, physical activity, avoidance of smoking, and maintenance of a healthy weight will help to reduce the risk of heart disease.

[112]http://www.mass.gov/Eeohhs2/docs/dph/substance_abuse/prevention_advice_moderate_drinking_safe.pdf (accessed May 2010).
[113] Rosen, Maggie. Drink to This. *Health Science Boston Globe*. April 6, 2004

- An Addiction Specialist and Senior Scientist at the Centre for Addiction and Mental Health at the University of Toronto states that "the health benefits of alcohol use are generally overstated and are virtually non-existent for young people. Even small amounts of alcohol increase the risk of injury and boost the chances of developing about sixty diseases."[114]

- The World Health Organization suggests that when differences relating to the individual's social and economic position are corrected, the seeming cardio-protective effects may no longer be found.[115]

- The most recent studies do not necessarily account for crucial, personal differences which greatly affect how alcohol reacts to the body. (See Personal Factors below.)

- Adults should talk to their health care providers before changing their drinking habits.

What Personal Factors Contribute to Reactions with Alcohol?

- Gender – Moderate drinking levels differ for men and women. This is because women's bodies process alcohol differently, and they are more sensitive to alcohol use.[116]

- Age – There are no safe limits of alcohol use for youth or adolescents. Consumption of alcohol under the age of 21 is

[114] Rehn, Jurgen, et al. *Alcohol as Damaging as Tobacco*. Nature. April 8, 2004.
[115] National Institute on Alcohol Abuse and Alcoholism. Alcohol Alert. No.16 PH 315. April, 1992.
[116] The World Health Organization. The Issue. Health Evidence Network. 2005.

illegal. Older adults, in addition, are much more sensitive to alcohol intake.[117]

- Personal and Family History – People with a personal or family history of alcohol problems or alcoholism must be especially cautious as they may not be able to drink alcohol safely.

- Medication Intake – Alcohol can interact with some prescription and over-the-counter medication. It is essential to ask individual health care providers before changing drinking patterns.[118]

- Pregnancy – Alcohol consumption during pregnancy can seriously affect the mental and physical development of the unborn baby. According to the Health and Nutrition Newsletter of Tufts University, alcoholic beverages should not be consumed by women of childbearing age who may become pregnant or pregnant and lactating women.[119]

What is "Moderate Drinking"?

- According to the World Health Organization, "there may be some danger that talking about a 'safe limit' (for alcohol use) will encourage more of the population to drink and spur light drinkers to drink up to the stated limit."[120]

---

[117] Rehn, Jurgen, et al. *Alcohol as Damaging as Tobacco.* Nature. April 8, 2004.

[118] Massachusetts Department of Public Health, Bureau of Substance Abuse Services and Bureau of Family and Community Health, The Massachusetts Health Promotion Clearinghouse of The Medical Foundation. **Healthy Aging: Medications and Alcohol**.

[119] *Dietary Guidelines for Americans, 2005.* Retrieved from: www.health.gov 2/16/05.

[120] National Institute on Alcohol Abuse and Alcoholism. Alcohol Alert. No.16 PH 315. April, 1992.

- Moderate drinking levels are generally defined as no more than one drink per day for women (under age 65) and no more than two drinks per day for men (under 65). These limits are based on differences between the sexes in both weight and metabolism. [121]

- Elderly (above age 65) should limit alcohol intake because their bodies process alcohol differently. The maximum limits of drinks a day for men over 65 is 1 drink per day, and for women over 65 is less than one per day. [122]

- There are no safe limits for alcohol use by youth.

- People with certain diseases, or who are taking over-the-counter or prescription medication should check with their pharmacist or health care provider, as even low levels of alcohol use may cause a reaction.

- The personal factors listed above can change the effects of even moderate levels of alcohol use.

What Are Potential Consequences of Alcohol Use?

Health Related Problems[123]

- liver cirrhosis
- elevated blood pressure
- variety of types of cancer
- stroke
- damage to unborn children.

---

[121] The World Health Organization. The Issue. Health Evidence Network. 2005.

[122] Massachusetts Department of Public Health, Bureau of Substance Abuse Services and Bureau of Family and Community Health, The Massachusetts Health Promotion Clearinghouse of The Medical Foundation. **Healthy Aging: Medications and Alcohol**.

[123] Dietary Guidelines for Americans, 2005. Retrieved from: www.health.gov 2/16/05.

Social, Legal and Safety Issues

- increased risk of family, work and other problems
- negative behavior modeling (parents setting examples for youth)
- absenteeism, low productivity
- financial hardship
- criminal behavior
- violence and/or accidental death
- driving under the influence of alcohol

Society at Large

- "In addition to the potential individual consequences of increased alcohol consumption, the public may suffer from the promotion of moderate drinking."[124]
- "Although drinking is a personal act and an individual responsibility, it is also behavior shaped by our societies and something for which society as a whole has responsibility."[125]
- According to the World Health Organization, "measures that influence drinkers in general will also have an impact on heavier drinkers. Promoting increased levels of moderate drinking may in turn increase overall consumption, even for those who should not do so."[126]

---

[124] Edwards, Griffith. *Alcohol policy: securing a positive impact on health.* Retrieved rom:www.euro.who.int/mediacentre/PressBackgrounders/2001/200110022 1/26/05.

[125] *Ibid.*

[126] National Institute on Alcohol Abuse and Alcoholism. *Alcohol Alert.* No.16 PH 315. April, 1992.

Appendix III

About Alcohol Abuse

About Alcohol Abuse[127]

Alcohol Abuse Facts

One of the key alcohol abuse facts or info about alcohol abuse is this: alcohol abuse is a pattern of drinking that can result in physical injury; ongoing alcohol-related relationship problems; the failure to attend to important responsibilities at school, work, or at home; and/or the experience of recurring alcohol-related legal problems (such as receiving multiple DWIs and DUIs) during a twelvemonth time period.

Another one of the key facts on alcohol abuse and some basic alcohol abuse information is that irresponsible and long term alcohol abuse usually results in various alcohol long term effects that are highly correlated with different diseases, medical issues, and illnesses. Stated differently, repetitive abusive drinking typically results in a number of alcohol long term effects that manifest themselves as alcohol abuse and alcoholism problems

Yet another one of the alcohol abuse facts and a bit of bottom line alcohol abuse information that many people do not realize is that binge drinking, even if done only a few times per year, is a form of alcohol abuse.

What is worse, apparently many people do not comprehend that binge drinking can and does result in alcohol poisoning, which, in some

---

[127] I am including this appendix, not to detract from my main argument against moderate drinking, but in fact to show the gravity of the problems to which moderate drinking exposes people. Though this article was not written from a Christian perspective, some of the facts that are given make it worth including. Courtesy of Integrity Business Systems and Solutions, c/o About Alcohol Abuse, 755 Broadway Avenue, Suite #4 Bedford, Ohio 44146 http://www.about-alcohol-abuse.com.

instances, can be fatal. Such alcohol abuse signs and information about alcohol abuse, binge drinking, and alcohol poisoning, it is asserted, needs to be taught to every student in our school system.

If you engage in abusive drinking you could be gambling with your life. How? Simply this: Many individuals, who drink excessively, involve themselves in binge drinking. And abusing alcohol in any fashion and long term alcohol abuse can eventually result in alcohol dependence which is a type of drug addiction.

As a consequence, why not break the connection between abuse and alcohol in your life, get some relevant information about alcohol facts and about alcohol abuse, and do some "proactive thinking" so that you can prevent the disease of alcoholism before it ever becomes an issue? In short, why not avoid any potentially unhealthy alcohol abuse effects, alcohol abuse "signs," and long term alcohol abuse and consider getting the alcohol abuse treatment that you need?

Alcohol Abuse Facts: What is Alcohol Abuse?

Many people think that alcohol abuse and alcoholism are the same. This information is not based on alcoholism facts, alcohol abuse facts, or about alcohol facts. Indeed, though both alcohol abuse and alcoholism are similar in that both point to the unfortunate connection that exists between abuse and alcohol, alcohol abuse, unlike alcoholism, does not include the loss of control due to drinking, physical dependence, or an extremely strong craving for alcohol.

Definition of Alcohol Abuse. Alcohol abuse is defined as a pattern of drinking that results in one or more of the following circumstances in a twelve-month time frame:

✓ Drinking in situations that can result in physical injury such as operating machinery.

✓ Continued drinking in spite of ongoing relationship problems that are the result of drinking.

✓ Failure to attend to important responsibilities at home, work, or school.

✓ Experiencing recurring alcohol-related legal problems. Examples include getting arrested for damaging someone's property, receiving a DUI, or for physically hurting someone while drunk.

An intelligent way of looking at the components that make up the definition of alcohol abuse is this: when a person exhibits problems in any or all of these areas consider this information as alcohol abuse signs. That is, the manifestation of any or all of these issues is often a red flag that the person is engaging in abusive drinking.

A Definition of Alcoholism

To understand the differences between alcohol abuse and alcoholism, we will provide a definition of alcoholism. According to alcoholism facts, alcoholism, also known as alcohol addiction or alcohol dependence, is a form of drug addiction and is a disease that includes the following symptoms:

✓ **Loss of control:** The inability to limit one's drinking over time or on any given occasion.

✓ **Craving**: A strong and continuing compulsion or need to drink.

✓ **Tolerance**: The need to drink increasing amounts of alcohol in order to "feel the buzz" or to "get high."

✓ **Physical dependence**: alcohol withdrawal symptoms when a person stops drinking after a period of excessive drinking. Such symptoms include: "the shakes," nausea, anxiety, and sweating.

When looking at alcohol abuse and alcoholism one key factor is worth mentioning. The longer a person engages in alcohol abuse, the higher the probability that he or she will eventually become alcohol dependent. Stated differently, those who engage in long term alcohol abuse are increasing their risk of becoming an alcoholic down the road.

Facts on Alcohol: Causes of Alcohol Abuse and Alcoholism

A question that has entered the minds of many people is the following: why can some individuals drink alcohol without encountering any difficulties or negative consequences while others cannot? Stated differently, what is about alcohol that leads some people to abuse and addiction while for others, enjoyment and moderation prevail? One answer to this question concerns genetics.

More to the point, according to the facts on alcohol abuse, researchers have found that having an alcoholic family member increases the risk of developing alcohol abuse or alcoholism.

In fact, there may be a genetic predisposition for certain people becoming "problem drinkers." In addition, research scientists have discovered that various environment factors can interact with one's genetics--the result being that both of these components can influence the development of alcohol related difficulties such as alcohol abuse. Examples of these environmental aspects include where and how a person lives, a person's culture, peer influences, the relative ease of obtaining alcohol, and one's family and friends.

Regrettably, once alcohol abuse starts, the behavior in many instances continues and can result in long term health, legal and social difficulties, and other types of alcohol abuse problems. Also unfortunate is the number of documented cases of adolescent alcohol abuse and youth alcohol abuse, especially the abuse of alcohol that takes place in high schools and on college campuses.

Information about Alcohol Abuse Facts and Alcoholism Statistics

There are certain words that almost always go together. Examples include the following: peanut butter and jelly, ham and cheese, and unfortunately, abuse and alcohol. Regrettably, the widespread dangers and destruction of alcohol abuse and alcoholism do not necessarily make a full impact on people until they are introduced to relevant statistics. As a result, we decided to include a few highly significant alcoholism statistics and alcohol abuse statistics.

Such alcohol abuse information, "alcohol abuse signs," and alcoholism facts, it is asserted, will not only help put alcohol abuse and alcoholism in a more understandable perspective, but it might help lead to more effective alcohol abuse prevention. Concerning alcohol abuse statistics and basic alcohol facts and info about alcohol abuse, according to a study undertaken by The National Center on Addiction and Substance Abuse (CASA) at Columbia University in 2005, the following alcohol abuse statistics and alcoholism statistics were discovered:

✓ According to alcohol abuse and alcoholism facts uncovered by alcohol research, American youth who drinking before the age 15 are four times more likely to become alcoholics than young people who do not drink before the age of 21. This statistic focuses on the importance of drinking at a later rather than at an earlier age. This statistics also points out very clearly how abuse and alcohol go together, even for teenagers.

✓ The 25.9% of underage drinkers who are alcohol abusers and alcohol dependent drink 47.3% of the alcohol that is consumed by all underage drinkers.

✓ Every day in the U.S. more than 13,000 children and teens take their first drink. Among other things, this means that many of these teens will understand first-hand the relationship between abuse and alcohol.

✓ Every year, 1400 American college students between the ages of 18 and 24 die from alcohol-related accidents and injuries, including motor vehicle accidents. Traffic fatalities, perhaps more than any other statistics, point out the devastating realities that often result from alcohol abuse and alcoholism.

✓ In the United States during 2004, 16,694 deaths occurred as a result of alcohol-related motor-vehicle crashes. This amount was approximately 39% of all traffic fatalities. This amounts to one alcohol-related death every 31 minutes. This statistic, quite honestly, is overwhelming. Talk about abuse and alcohol--one alcohol related traffic fatality every 31 minutes and the grief and devastation suffered from these deaths is beyond comprehension.

✓ Here's one of the alcohol abuse and alcoholism facts and an alcohol statistic that though logical, is something that most drinkers and non-drinkers probably do not know: The 9.6% of adult alcoholics drink 25% of the alcohol that is consumed by all adult drinkers.

✓ Every year in the U.S. more than 150,000 college students develop health problems that are alcohol-related. This is additional evidence that alcohol abuse and alcoholism, unfortunately, are intimately interrelated to one another.

✓ Alcohol abuse and alcoholism cost the United States an estimated $220 billion in 2005. This dollar amount was more than the cost associated with cancer ($196 billion) and obesity ($133 billion). Though dollar amounts like this are hard to comprehend, at least they make an attempt at placing a dollar value on the relationship of abuse and alcohol.

Alcohol Abuse: Facts about Binge Drinking

Here are some more important facts on alcohol abuse, alcohol abuse information, and alcohol abuse signs. It appears that many people do not understand that getting drunk "only" once or twice per year is neither "drinking in moderation" nor "responsible drinking." In fact, there is a term for this kind of occasional alcohol abuse: binge drinking.

Binge drinking is defined as having four or more drinks at one sitting for women and five or more drinks at one sitting for men. Stated another way, when an individual consumes an excessive amount of alcohol over a short period of time, or abuse is continuous over a number of days or weeks, this is called intensive use, bingeing, or binge drinking.

Obviously, binge drinking perfectly illustrates the relationship that exists between abuse and alcohol and is one of the most dangerous alcohol abuse problems that a person can experience.

It is interesting to note that hangovers are frequently more common in light to moderate drinkers than in heavy and chronic drinkers, suggesting that binge drinking can be as threatening as chronic drinking. Therefore any man who drinks more than five drinks or any woman who has more than four drinks in one sitting is at risk for a hangover. When used intelligently, such alcohol abuse signs can help prevent abusive drinking as well as hangovers.

Binge drinking not only significantly increases the risk of injury and contracting sexually transmitted diseases, but it can also result in alcohol poisoning. Considering the fact that 60 percent of American men between the ages of 18 and 25 binge drink and in 2002, a reported 2.6 million U.S. binge drinkers were between the ages of 12 and 17, binge drinking is not only extremely dangerous and potentially fatal, but it is also a drinking pattern that affects millions of teens, pre-teens, and young adults. To state the obvious, people who regularly engage in binge drinking need alcohol abuse help because they are actively engaging in abusive drinking.

SELECT BIBLIOGRAPHY

BOOKS and ARTICLES:

Bacchiocchi, Samuele. *Wine in the Bible: A Biblical Study on the Use of Alcoholic Beverages.* Berrien Springs, MI: Biblical Perspectives, 1989. [Seventh-day Adventist]

Clarke, Adam. *Commentary, Genesis 40:11.*

Emmons, *His Word is Truth,* Israel My Glory, Jan/Feb 2009

Field, Leon C. *Oinos: a Discussion of the Bible Wine Question.* New York: Phillips & Hunt. 1883. Harvard College Library, digitalized by Google. http://books.google.com/books.

Jaeggli, Randy. *The Christian and Drinking, a Biblical Perspective on Moderation and Abstinence.* Greenville, SC: BJU Press. 2008. This book has been withdrawn from publication.

Josephus, *Antiquities of the Jews,* Book 2, Chapter 5.

Kirton, John W. *The Water Drinkers of the Bible.* Edinburgh: Lorimer and Gillies, 1885. Harvard University Library, digitalized by Google. http://books.google.com/books.

Lumpkins, Peter. *Alcohol Today: Abstinence in an age of Indulgence,* Hannibal Books, Garland Texas, 2009

Marshall, John George. *Strong Drink Delusion, with its Criminal and Ruinous Results Exposed.* Halifax: the Journal Office, 1855.

McGuiggan, Jim. *The Bible, the Saint, & the Liquor Industry.* Lubbock, TX: International Biblical Resources Inc, 1977.

Milner, Duncan C., *Lincoln and Liquor,* The Neale Publishing Company, 440 Fourth Avenue, New York, 1920, p. 15.

137

Nott, Eliphalet. *Lectures on Temperance*, NEW-YORK: SHELDON, BLAKEMAN & CO., 115 NASSAU STREET, 1857, pp. 53,54.

Patton, William. *The Laws of Fermentation and the Wines of the Ancients.* New York: National Temperance Society and Publishing House, 1871.

Peterson, Ivan. *Let me call thee Devil.* Available from petersonministries.com

Rosen, Maggie. *Drink to This.* Health Science Boston Globe. April 6, 2004

Stott, John. *Evangelical Truth* (Downers Grove, IL.: InterVarsity Press, 1999), pp. 116-117.

Teachout, Raymond L., *Adrift from the Gospel*, (Chateau-Richer, Quebec, EBPA, 2011), p. 149.

Teachout, Robert. *Wine the Biblical Imperative: Total Abstinence.* Detroit, MI: Published by Author, 1983.

Thompson, *The Hand of God in American History*, p. 559, cited in Milner, Duncan C., "Lincoln and Liquor," The Neale Publishing Company, 440 Fourth Avenue, New York, 1920, p.13.

Van Lob, Muriel. *Alcohol in the Bible*, Three Book series. Canistota, SD: Promise House Publishers, 1993.

Van Impe, Jack. *Alcohol, the Beloved Enemy.* Nashville: Thomas Nelson Publishers, 1980.

PRINT:

Reinstadler, Kym. 'Thou Shalt Not' Revoked. *The Grand Rapids Press.* Nov 21, 2009.

INTERNET:

http://aa-nia-dist11.org/Documents/roots2.pdf (Accessed 12/13/2010).

138

http://abcnews.go.com/GMA/Health/Story?id=2065494&page=1 (accessed: 8/5/2009).

www.alcoholcontents.com (accessed: 8/5/2009)

http://www.alcoholism-information.com/Alcoholism_Statistics.html, (Accessed 7/7/2011).

http://www.aletheiabaptistministries.org/ (accessed 9/2/2011).

www.amazon.com/Guerzoni-Biodynamic-Mosto-Grape-Juice/dp/B0000U3BG0 (Accessed 3/29/11).http://www.apologeticspress.org/articles/2293 Apologetics Press: Scripturally Speaking- The Bible is its Own Best Interpreter. (Accessed 12/2010)

http://www.amethystinitiative.org. (Accessed 6/28/2011).

http://www.ancient-hebrew.org/20_interpretation.html (Accessed 7/30/2011) "The Eight Rules of Interpretation," Guy Duty.

http://www.apologeticspress.org/articles/2293 (Accessed 12/2010)

http://articles.cnn.com/2000-03-31/health/wine.heart.wmd_1_grape-juice-nonalcoholic-wine-john-folts?_s=PM:HEALTH. Accessed 9/22/2011.

www.associatedcontent.com/article/784631/ wasjesusa brewer.html?singlepage=true&cat=22 (accessed: 9/30/2009).

www.aventureuse- balade.net/reportages/raisin.html (accessed: 8/5/2009)

www.biblestudy.org/basicart/does- bible-permit-drinking-wine-alcohol.html (accessed: 8/5/2009)

www.biblicalperspectives.com/books/wine_in_the_bible/1.html (accessed: 8/5/2009)

http://blog.chron.com/believeitornot/2010/07/pour-one-for-the-pastor-evangelical-perspectives-on-alcohol-and-the-church/ (Accessed 6/28/2011)

http://blog.davidrhoades.org /2008_06_01_ archive.html. (Accessed 7/31/2011).

http://books.google.com/books Leon C.Field, Oinos: a discussion of the Bible Wine Question (A.M., New York: Phillips & Hunt), pp. 17, 18. From Harvard College Library, digitalized by Google. (accessed 1/24/2010).

http://books.google.com/books?id=FrYaAAAAYAAJ&pg=PA51&lpg=PA51&dq=the+water+drinkers+of+the+bible&source=bl&ots=gXRbUoD15e&sig=YEiV59q5FWD8AwjdZK2AbtIOzAY&hl=en&ei=JnEwTpSBPMu4tge k_tyjCQ&sa=X&oi=book_result&ct=result&resnum=5&ved=0CDoQ6AEwBA#v=onepage&q&f=false [John W. Kirton, The Water Drinkers of the Bible, LLD, Edinburgh: Lorimer and Gillies,1885, p. 61. Preserved by Harvard University Library and put on the web by Google.com. (Accessed 1/25.2010].

http://www.bpnews.net/bpfirstperson.asp?id=25221 Norm Miller, Alcohol, Acts 29 and the SBC. Posted on Mar 20, 2007 (Accessed 6/23/2011).

www.camy.org/factsheets/index.php?FactsheetID.

http://www.cato.org/pub display.php?pub_id=1017, (Accessed 7/22/2011).

www.churchhistory101.com/docs/Wine-Ancient-World.pdf, R.A. Baker, Wine in the Ancient World, (accessed 10/13/09)

www.churchhistory101.com/docs/Wine-Ancient-World.pdf (accessed: 10/13/2009).

140

http://www.cnn.com/2010 /HEALTH/11/01/alcohol.harm/index.html
By the CNN Wire Staff, November 1, 2010 1:14 p.m. EDT.
(Accessed 4/15/2011).

http://www.come-over.to/FAS/alcdeath.htm, (Accessed 7/7/2011).

http://www.ecstasyaddiction.com/PressReleasePages/therealcostofalco
holadvertising.html (Accessed 4/15/2011).

http://en.wikipedia.org/wiki/American_Temperance_Society.
(Accessed 12/11/2010).

http://en.wikipedia.org/wiki/Defrutum (Accessed 8/5/2011).

www.focusas.com/Alcohol.html (accessed: 8/5/2009).

http://www.ftc.gov/reports/alcohol/appendixb.shtm (Accessed
4/15/2011).

http://books.google.com/books?id=-iMIZ-S82v4C&pg=PA195&-
lpg=PA195&dq=REVIEW+OF+DR.+CROSBY%27S+%22C
ALM+VIEW+OP+TEMPERANCE.&source=bl&ots=npAWu
3sIj&sig=iHxyXjFVguGotwghzzuaNe1UrP0&hl=en&ei=zpd4
Tv6oOMbjsQL_x_2uDQ&sa=X&oi=book_result&ct=result&r
esnum=1&ved=0CCAQ6AEwAA#v=onepage&q=REVIEW%
20OF%20DR.%20CROSBY%27S%20%22CALM%20VIEW
%20OP%20TEMPERANCE.&f=false (Accessed 7/28/2011).

http://books.google.com/books?id=GpgOAAAAYAAJ&printsec=front
cover&dq=Personal+Narratives+with+Reflections+and+Rema
rks&hl=en&ei=9AczTq68CdGhtwfl_eGZDQ&sa=X&oi=book
_result&ct=result&resnum=1&ved=0CCkQ6AEwAA#v=onep
age&q&f=false "Personal Narratives with Reflections and
Remarks," Halifax, N.S. T Chamberlain, 176 Argyle St 1866,
Harvard College, Google e-books. (Accessed 7/28/2011).

http://www.foi.org/ godistrueandtruth . (Accessed 7/28/2011).

http://www.google.com/search?q=definition+of+context&ie=utf8&oe= utf-wikipedia8&aq=t&rls=org.mozilla:en- US:official&client=firefox-a, (Accessed 8/10/2011).

http://www.google.com/search?q=Summit+I+of+the+International+Co uncil+on+Biblical+Inerrancy+took+place+in+Chicago+on+Oc tober+26- 28%2C+1978+for+the+purpose+of+affirming+ afresh+the+doctrine+of+the+inerrancy+of+Scripture&ie=utf- 8&oe=utf-8&aq=t&rls=org.mozilla:en-US:official&client= firefox-a Summit I of the International Council on Biblical Inerrancy took place in Chicago on October 26-28, 1978 for the purpose of affirming afresh the doctrine of the inerrancy of Scripture... Explaining Hermeneutics: A Commentary on the Chicago Statement on Biblical Hermeneutics. Oakland, California: International Council on Biblical Inerrancy, 1983.

https://mail.google.com/mail/?hl=en&shva=1#contact/group/1ddba968 9c455af/anewwinebook/7840fead88cca462 (Accessed 12/07/2010).

http://www.islamqa.com/en/ref/127938. (accessed: 8/5/2009).

http://www.huffingtonpost.com/2011/02/11/alcohol-related-deaths- _n_821900.html, (Accessed 7/7/2011).

http://lincoln.lib.niu.edu/digitalreform.html (Accessed 12/13/2010).

http://machaut.uchicago.edu/?resource=Webster%27s&word=wine&us e1913=on&use1828=on (accessed 10/29/09).

www.mass.gov/...abuse/prevention_advice_moderate_drinking_safe.rtf (Accessed 6/28/2011).

http://www.mayoclinic.com/health/alcohol/SC00024, (Accessed 6/28/2011).www.islamqa.com/en/ref/127938 (accessed: 8/5/2009).

http://www.medicalnewstoday.com/articles/206300.php, (Accessed 7/7/2011).

http://www.msnbc.msn.com/id/39938704/ns/health-
  addictions/t/alcohol-more-dangerous-heroin-cocaine-study-
  finds/ MARIA CHENG, *The Associated Press*, Sunday,
  October 31, 2010; 8:08 PM (Accessed 4/15/2011).

www.ncadd.org/facts/numberoneprob.html (accessed: 8/5/2009).

http://prohibitionhangover.com/israelwine.html (Accessed
  12/07/2010).http://www.reuters.com/article/2010/11/01/us-
  drugs-alcohol-idUSTRE6A000O20101101. Published
  November 01, 2010, Reuters. (Accessed 4/15/2011).

http://www.renewamerica.com/columns/creech/051122, (Accessed
  7/8/2011).

http://www.reuters.com/article/2010/11/01/us-drugs-alcohol-
  idUSTRE6A000O20101101, (Accessed 7/7/2011).

http://www.studylight.org/com/acc/ view.cgi? book=ge&chapter=040.
  (Accessed 7/22/2011).

http://www.theologue.org/hermbiblicl-ramm.htm, (Accessed 12/2010).

http://www.time.com/time/magazine/article/0,9171,912518,00.html#ix
  zz1QIBrCUjP, (Accessed 6/25/2011).

http://www.unm.edu/~cosap/RESEARCH.HTM, (Accessed
  6/28/2011).

http://utc.iath.virginia.edu/sentimnt/sneslbat.html. {Accessed
  7/5/2011).

http://en.wikipedia.org/wiki/Must (Accessed 9/08/2011).

http://www.winemaking.com/; http://en.wikipedia.org/wiki/
  Winemaking (Accessed 12/06/2010).